Relief Carving
TREASURY

by William F. Judt

Fox Chapel Publishing Co., Inc.
1970 Broad Street
East Petersburg, PA 17520

© 1998 by Fox Chapel Publishing Company, Inc.

Publisher: Alan Giagnocavo
Project Editor: Ayleen Stellhorn
Desktop Specialist: Robert Altland, Altland Design
Cover Photography:

ISBN # 1–56523–097–3

To order your copy of this book,
please send check or money order
for cover price plus $2.50 to:

**Fox Chapel Books Orders
1970 Broad Street
East Petersburg, PA 17520**

Try your favorite book supplier first!

Manufactured in China

A friendly tip for woodcarvers

We would like to pass along information on the best deal we have ever seen for woodcarvers.

The National Woodcarvers Association is a non-profit organization dedicated to the art of woodcarving. Members receive six issues of "Chip Chats" a colorful magazine full of techniques, show happenings, photographs of masterworks and more.

We highly recommend that every carver from beginner to professional join -
you won't be disappointed!

Membership is only $11.00 per year ($14 outside the USA)
National Woodcarvers Association
7424 Miami Ave.
Cincinnati, OH 4543

Table of Contents

Introduction

What I Love About Relief

I love relief carving. There is no other form of carving that does for me what relief carving does. Whittling may be fun, sculpture may be lofty, chip carving is delicate, caricature is charming, but relief carving is the grandest of them all. It offers the artist a wooden canvas where shapes, textures, patterns, perspective, borders, text and even color can be used in harmony to render a theme or subject.

Even after over 22 years of carving in relief, I still cannot see any end to its pleasure. Having completed about 1,000 carvings in this time, most of which were commissions, I am also no closer to exhausting the possibilities that exist in relief carving than when I started carving in 1975. Thus, I have come to the conclusion that there is virtually no subject that cannot be carved in relief, and no end to the variety in which any one subject can be rendered.

The Problem with Relief

The problem with learning relief carving is that there are so few resources for it in comparison to the other forms of carving we see today. There are very few books on relief carving. There are very few courses being taught on relief carving. And certainly, there are very few sources for detailed, accurate and useful patterns for relief carving aimed at the experienced to advanced carver.

This book is my first attempt to remedy this deficiency. Other books will follow, focusing on tips and techniques for the relief carver and maybe even a step-by-step project to demonstrate certain skills and strategies. But this book will attempt to show you, using pictures and patterns, what is possible for the carver who is not a professional and whose artistic abilities are average.

Features of this Book

Recent developments in desktop computer technology, including scanners, powerful graphics software and online communications all contributed to my ability to produce this book. Five years ago, patterns of this quality would have been difficult to create. My carving classes have produced a number of excellent patterns over the years that have proven popular. These I wanted to put to use, combining accurate patterns with clear color photos, so that the carver can interpret the pattern using evidence found in the photo of the finished product.

The text portion of this book intends to put in words what can't be explained in pictures. Tool sizes, hints, cautions, strategies and procedure are all listed in the written instructions accompanying each pattern.

I resisted the temptation to produce a "how-to" or "step-by-step" book when I compiled these patterns. A step-by-step book requires many photographs of a single project. In the end, it guides you through the process of carving a single project.

With this book, I wanted to introduce you to a wider and more eclectic range of carvings in order to show you the diversity of this medium. In so doing, I am aware that the beginner will have a difficult time reproducing these carvings, even with the excellent patterns and beautiful photographs. Beginners can use this book to dream a little. The experienced and advanced carvers can use it to help them accomplish the task of creating a beautiful carving of their choice.

Acknowledgements

First I want to thank my wife Deborah for her unwavering support and encouragement for this project. She shared the enthusiasm I had for this first book and generously offered her critique and advice so that this book could be the best it could be.

My wife is a dancer. I am a carver. As part of our marriage arrangement, we agreed that I would not require her to carve if she would not require me to dance. We have kept our promises. But that does not mean we fail to share an appreciation for each other's artistic passion or an admiration for what the other has accomplished over the years in our respective crafts. I must confess that a carver's most valuable earthly resource is a loving and supportive spouse. That I have, and am grateful for it. The fact that she is beautiful, talented and good natured is a plus, wouldn't you agree?

I also want to acknowledge the contributions my students have made to this book. I am not referring only to those who allowed me to use their finished carvings as examples in this book. I refer to all my students over the years who have contributed to my education as a carver and as an instructor.

I have learned so much from my students that I cannot measure it all. While they were teaching me, they supplied part of my income as a carver and made it possible to work full time at my craft. Besides this, they have given me company on this journey we call life. Until I started teaching, I carved alone. With my wonderful students who share my enthusiasm for this craft, I am no longer alone. I thank each of them from the heart.

SOLA DEO GLORIA

Contributors

The students who have contributed to this book are: Laurette Cissel, Dennis McIntosh, Hans Dietrich, Bob Neufeld, Kevin Dewhirst, Neil Dobson, Ron Bush and Louw Smit.

The Internet Connection

Since 1995 I have enjoyed promoting woodcarving on the Internet. With my own website, where links can be found to most of the woodcarvers who are online, and with the Woodcarver Mailing List, where carvers from around the world meet to talk woodcarving, I have encouraged the growth and prosperity of an online carving community.

This has been a great pleasure and a profound privilege for me. To be there at the very start of it all,

from the day there was nothing of woodcarving on the Internet, to now, where we can find literally hundreds of websites and many times more woodcarvers online, I have witnessed the unprecedented explosion of interest in woodcarving on the Internet.

Over the next few years we will see carvers, suppliers, clubs, organizations, magazines, listserves, chat groups and maybe even conventions online, all with the common interest of carving among them. The internet allows carvers to meet and enjoy the company of other carvers from around the world quickly, inexpensively and daily.

If you are online, please feel free to email me at bjudt@terranet.ab.ca. Also, take time to visit my woodcarving website, the first carving website on the Internet. The URL is:

http://www.terranet.ab.ca/~bjudt/myhome.html

Along with my personal web page, I maintain an online Woodcarving E-zine called, appropriately, the WWWoodc@rver E-zine, which is published electronically on a bi-monthly basis. It contains articles and images of general interest to carvers worldwide. You can find it at the following URL:

http://www.terranet.ab.ca:80/~bjudt/WWWoodcarver/WWWoodcarver.html

Another very important online resource is the Woodcarver Mailing List, which allows carvers from around the world to communicate with each other on a daily basis and enjoy each other's company, expertise, tips and talents. You can access this mailing list at the following URL:

http://www.terranet.ab.ca:80/~bjudt/WoodcarverList.html

Both the E-zine and the Mailing List are free to access, but are supported by voluntary donations from subscribers.

With these links you will be able to connect into the entire woodcarving community online. See you online!

Before You Begin

The patterns in this book have all been carved by normal, average human beings. I bring this to your attention so you will know that each of these carving patterns is within your reach, maybe not all of them right now, but all of them eventually.

Most of the carvings in this book were carved by my students, who are adults from all walks of life. Welders, teachers, secretaries, retired farmers, truck drivers, forestry workers, parts persons, mechanics, salesmen and preachers have all contributed their work to this book.

It is my belief that if these ordinary people can carve these wonderful pieces, so can you. As it took time to learn the skills, patience to observe the patterns and time to execute these carvings, so it will take the same for you. In the end, you will manage to figure out how these carvings were done by observing the photos, studying the pattern and carefully reading the notes accompanying each pattern.

All the information you need is there. In fact, you will have more information at hand than the people who originally carved these pieces. They had to find their way to the balanced design, the proper shape and correct line. Sometimes it meant carving an area three or four times to get it just right. But you have the photos to guide you. Admittedly, they had an instructor close at hand, which you do not. So I suppose it balances out, doesn't it. In the end, you will learn much from these projects, this I can assure you.

Assumptions

This book was written for the experienced to advanced carver. It assumes you have at least a basic set of tools—for example, a set of 12 Swiss, or Henry Taylor or Stubai, or Marples tools plus a few incidental tools—and know how to keep them sharp.

You will already know how to use these tools: how to carve "with the grain," stop cut, rough out a panel, use a router and undercut. If you are deficient in any of these skills, seek the assistance of a friend or instructor. The effort to get up to speed in these areas will be worth your while.

It also assumes you have access to some shop equipment like a sturdy workbench, a bandsaw, a jointer, a planer and a router. You must have some bar clamps and C-clamps for the laminating process, a mallet to drive your tools through the hardwood, some carbon paper for tracing and access to a quality photocopier for enlarging the patterns. An alternative to the photocopier is a good pantograph or the patience to draw a grid system for enlarging the pattern to scale. Do not forget the coffee pot. Carving and coffee are natural companions. <Grin>

Keys to Good Relief Carving

1. Compression of depth

It is impossible to carve in relief without compressing the subject in the depth dimension. Width and height are normal dimensions in relief, but depth can be compressed as much as 50:1. Your average coin is a testament to how much the depth dimension can be compressed while still allowing you to carve a perfectly normal-looking relief. The patterns in this book rely on less compression than a coin, but still compression can be as much as 20:1, as in the "Wolf Portrait." There, for example, the eyeball, which is 1" wide, will need only $1/16$" depth to render it properly. This represents 16:1 compression.

2. Proper lighting

Relief carving needs light and shadow to reveal its beauty and perspective. You also need light and shadow to assist you while you carve just as much as the carving needs these when it is hanging on the wall. I use natural light as much as possible, coming from windows at 90° to each other, that is one window on my left and one straight ahead.

If windows cannot provide you with enough cross-lighting, then use artificial light, preferably a low-hanging florescent light on your left and another at the far end of your worktable. If these lights hang about 24" above the height of your worktable, you will receive the light and shadow you need to clearly see the details of your relief.

3. Safety

Sharp tools are at the same time dangerous to use and the greatest safety feature on your worktable. Sharp tools cut wood easily, and require less brute force to move them through the wood than dull tools, thus allowing you more control over them, and consequently, greater safety. Learn to keep your tools sharp.

But sharp is not everything. Proper cutting angles make a tool glide through the wood, while improper angles make it hard to keep the tool in the wood where it can do its job. Learn to shape your tools correctly.

An excellent guide for this is Leonard Lee's book *The Complete Guide to Sharpening.* I have seen this book and can vouch for its accuracy and clarity.

Two-handed carving is the only carving I teach. The two times I sliced my own hands were when I was holding the gouge with one hand, while supporting the carving with the other. If two hands are on the tool, the tool cannot possibly be in your flesh. In my carving classes, my students still get cut, but only while reaching for a tool in a tool pouch and cutting themselves inadvertently.

I charge a dollar for each drop of blood spilled on my floor, reasoning that blood on the floor is evidence that a student has not followed my safety guidelines. So far, I have not been able to assess any "blood" penalties against my students. <wide grin>

3. Using the right wood

Since you will be investing many hours in these carvings, take care to choose good quality wood for your project. Wood is the smallest cost component of any relief carving. Labor is responsible for your greatest investment. If wood costs $20, and you spend 40 hours on one of these carvings, you can see that labor is the most important consideration. So go for the best wood possible. You will be glad you did.

Coarse woods should be used only when they serve a definite purpose in your carving and enhance the final product. For the most part, coarse woods like oak have a grain pattern that competes with the relief for visibility. You want the relief to take center stage in all your carvings, so stick with close-grained woods with even coloring and subdued figure.

4. Carving Aids

If you wish to learn more quickly how to carve, and if you wish to benefit from the ingenuity and expertise of others, then join a carving club, take lessons, attend competitions and workshops and read books on carving. It is preferable if you do all of these.

Many carvers like myself started with carving classes, but suffered later under the effects of isolation from the carving community. Mind you, when I started carving twenty-two years ago there was not much community among carvers, especially in Canada. But there is a growing community of carvers these days, to the point where you can go to almost any town or city populated by more than 30,000 people and find instruction, clubs or both. These days there is a wealth of excellent books on the market to teach and illustrate the craft and art of carving. Make use of these resources. They will accelerate your growth as a carver immensely.

General Tips and Techniques

Laminating

1. Select seasoned wood that is clear of knots and heartwood and free of checks and cracks.

2. Build some camber into your panels to help control the tendency of the panel to cup to the carved side. For a complete technical explanation of this procedure, along with illustrations, see the May-June 1995 issue of *Chip Chats* magazine, pages 4, 5 and 6. There you will find the article discussing the use of camber in the laminating process.

3. Be very sure that you place the center vertical line of the pattern parallel to the nearest joint of the panel. Otherwise when the carving is finished and displayed on the wall, it will always appear to hang crooked. Take care also, to ensure that the side grain of the wood rises from bottom to top and that your laminations are vertical rather than horizontal whenever possible. This makes for a more attractive carving.

4. Keep your shop warm. Temperatures less than 20°C (70°F) at bench level will allow the glue to set properly. Temperatures that get as low as 10°C (50°F) put the gluing process at risk.

Routering

As with all reliefs, it is possible to use the router to establish levels accurately and to greatly reduce the amount of time needed to "waste" the background wood. Don't worry about leaving router marks on the carving. You will carve all evidence of the routering out of the carving before you are finished.

A plunge router is the only type of router I recommend for this procedure, as it allows the safe and controlled vertical entry and exit of the bit from the wood. They are also generally more powerful and heavier, both desirable attributes when it comes to using them for relief work.

Routering depths are indicated on the patterns. These, of course, indicate depth from the top surface of the panel. For example, the symbol "1/4" indicates a depth of $1/4"$ from the top level of the panel. These depths represent the highest point in any given area, not the lowest.

Bevels

A bevel is a flat cut, at an angle between 45° and 60° from horizontal, that is applied to a sharp edge in order to strengthen the edge and to tilt it toward the viewer. The idea here is that sharp edges are hard to see from the position of the viewer who is standing in front of the carving.

Bevels allow light from the side to hit the edge and bounce forward to the viewer's eye

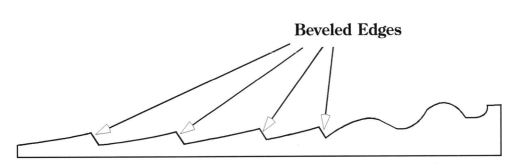

Beveled Edges

Bevel Cross Section

where it is interpreted as a line of light. Where bevels catch shadow, they appear to the viewer as dark lines around a shape or area. Both the line of light and the line of shadow help define an edge that would otherwise be hard to see, adding definition and clarity to your carvings.

All the carvings in this book employ bevels, some more than others. Among the best examples in this book are the carvings titled "Ascending Lord," "Eagle Landscape" and "Jesus and the Children." Inspect and study these carvings to see the effect bevels have on them.

Undercutting

Undercutting is the process of carving the edge of a figure/shape so that the uncarved portion, what could be referred to as the "behind" part of the figure, is removed from view. This involves angling your tool so that it cuts the edge at 20° off vertical. The top of the edge will subsequently overhang the bottom of the edge by that angle.

Undercutting transforms a shape from two-dimensional to three-dimensional in very short order. It is relatively easy to do. When the viewer cannot see the flat, unattractive side of a figure, his brain tells him that the figure must be round. Thus, undercutting is a trick relief carvers use to assist in developing shape and perspective in their carvings.

Properly done, an undercut will leave a continuous, smooth stop cut around the base of your figure and a smooth, angled surface under the edge.

Stamping

Of all the textures at the disposal of the relief carver, none draws more comment than stamping. I can exhibit a finished carving to the public and be assured that one of the first questions I will be asked is "How did you do this?" referring, of course, to the stamped areas of the carving. People have to touch it to make sure it is real.

Stamping Tool Detail

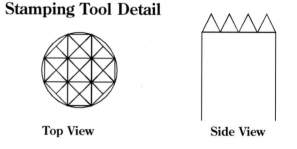

Top View   **Side View**

Stamping removes all reflection from a surface, leaving it to appear darker than the surrounding wood. Stamping also helps to hide defects like orphaned stop-cuts and slightly uneven background levels. I like to say that stamping covers a multitude of woodcarving sins.

You will probably have to make your own

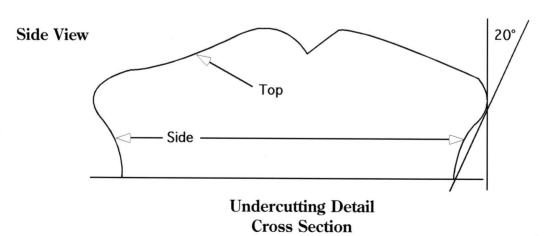

Side View   20°

Top

Side

Undercutting Detail
Cross Section

stamping tools. Simply described, they consist of a cross-hatch pattern of points filed into the end of a bolt, which, when struck by a hammer, punctures the surface of the wood, leaving small, randomly dispersed holes over the surface of the wood.

The cross-hatch is made with a $1/4$" triangle file. The points need only be separated by $1/16$" in straight, even rows. The tool is used by rotating it slightly each time it is struck into the wood, leaving a randomly distributed series of holes in the wood.

The bolts used can range from $1/8$" wide to $1/2$" wide, small ones for small spaces and large ones for wide-open spaces.

Finishing: The SSW Method

SSW stands for Sanding Sealer/Wax. By far the best finish I have ever had the pleasure of using involves a base-coat of quick-dry sanding sealer followed by the application of a "000" steel wool (or a fine abrasive pad used by woodworkers to smooth the surface) and finished with a top-coat of hardwood paste wax.

Sanding sealer is a specialty product that is available in most paint stores. It is applied with a brush, soaks into the wood and dries to the touch in 10 minutes (recoats dry in 4–6 hours). It effectively seals the wood and brings out the wood's inner beauty.

Sanding sealer is a clear finish. Because sanding sealer soaks in, it does not easily puddle in low spots, corners and tight places, unless you drench an area. Because it is a soft finish, any runs can be removed with steel wool prior to applying a wax topcoat. Because it dries quickly, you can work with it more easily. By itself, sanding sealer is absorbed into the wood unevenly, depending on the porosity of the wood, that is, whether it is put on the flat side (less porous) or on the end grain (more porous). The result is that, initially, your relief carving, with only sanding sealer on it, will look rather dull, some parts shiny

and others flat. This is where the steel wool comes in. Take your "000" steel wool and evenly rub the entire carving (except, perhaps rough or stamped areas) until all particulates stuck in the finish are removed, along with brush hairs and the like. The idea is to "scuff" the sanding sealer evenly in preparation for the application of the paste wax. Paste wax is what puts the shine back onto the relief carving.

To use the SSW method, apply the sanding sealer evenly over the carving, back first, then sides, then the front. Let the finish dry overnight. Next day, steel-wool the carving, taking care to be vigorous enough to remove imperfections like dust particles and runs, but not so vigorous as to remove wood or erode the crisp toolmarking you worked so hard to achieve. Then vacuum and wipe the carving thoroughly, so there is no trace of dust, steel wool particles or grit remaining. Then apply an even (not thick) coat of paste wax (suitable for hardwood floors, not liquid wax) over the areas that you previously had "scuffed" with the steel wool. Use a soft cloth to apply the wax.

Now, use a pure, soft, bristle brush to buff the wax, removing any excess wax from cracks and corners. Finally, get a clean, soft cloth (like a clean baby diaper) and polish the carving until it shines.

The result will be a soft, even, smooth-to-the-touch finish that will be the envy of your carving colleagues. This finish will invite touching, but don't worry, because the top coat of wax resists finger prints. Let people feel how smooth the surface of your carving is. To clean your carving in the years ahead, simply vacuum the carving with a soft vacuum brush and wipe with a soft, dry cloth. Do not re-apply wax, especially spray waxes. Do not use a damp cloth to dust your carving. This finish is designed to last for decades.

Finishing: Shoe Polishes

A solid alternative to the SSW method is the use of shoe polishes. I use the newer "shoe creams" available in a multitude of colors. They contain a heavy measure of pigment suspended in a soft wax paste. Applied with a tooth brush and buffed with a clean bristle brush (to spread and polish the pigmented wax), and then buffed with a soft cloth, shoe cream gives the wood a soft, even finish over the entire carving.

Advantages of this finish are many. It is a one-step finish. It is easy and fast to apply. As long as you make sure that none of the polish dries before you have a chance to brush it out, and you are careful to clean excess polish from corners and cracks, this product is hard to misuse.

Unknown to many, shoe polish adheres to the surface of your relief unevenly. This means that on flat grain, little of it adheres, leaving the wood to show through more. On cross-grain and end-grain, polish adheres more heavily because of the increased porosity of these surfaces, making the wood look darker or more colorful. This is not a problem, because the differences in surface adhesion make for subtle gradations of color intensity over the carving, with some surprisingly beautiful effects.

Polish also tends to hide defects, such as the color differences between pieces of wood that are glued side by side and mineral streaks that sometimes appear in the most awkward places in a carving. If the wood will not look absolutely beautiful with a clear finish (my preference), then use your favorite shoe (cream) polish. But try the polish on a spare piece of relief carving first, just to get the hang of it.

Enjoy!

Gallery

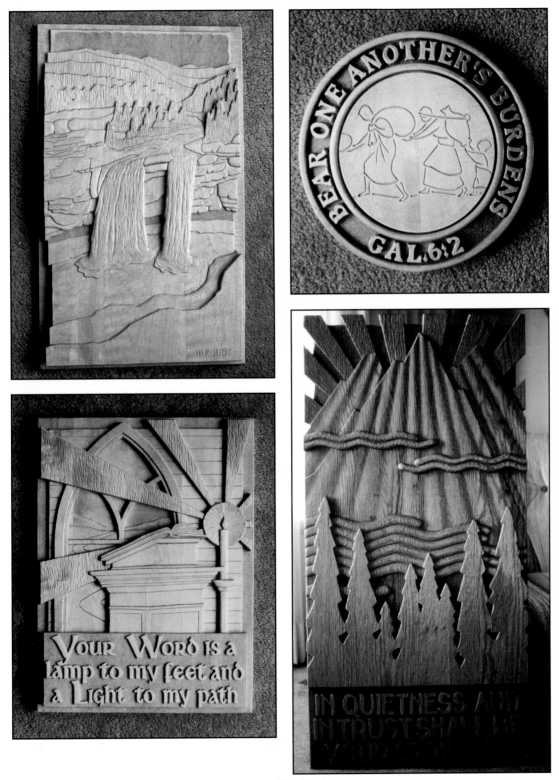

Clockwise from upper-left: *Kakwa Falls*, 18" x 27", White Birch
Bear One Another's Burdens, 14 ¹/₂" diameter, Hard Maple
In Quietness and Trust..., 24" x 48", Red Oak
Your Word is a Lamp..., 18" x 24", White Birch

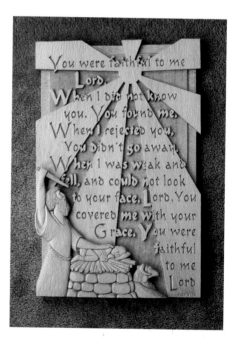

Clockwise from upper-left:
Peace Country Classic, 18" diameter,
White Birch

Canada Geese, 22" x 33", Hard Maple

Behold, I am the Handmaid..., 16" x 24",
Eastern (yellow) Birch

You were faithful to me Lord..., 20" x 30",
White Birch

Environmental Award, 22" x 32", White Birch
Capture a Dream, 1994, 18" x 22", White Birch
Lo I Am With You Always..., 15" x 19", Hard Maple

Clockwise from upper-left:
Semper Fidelis, 30" x 48", Red Oak
Deer Landscape, 22" x 30", White Birch
Rooster, 12½" x 18", White Birch
Old House, 24" x 24", White Birch

Sailing Ship

Artist: Hans Dietrich
Dimensions: 12" by 14½"
Wood: White Birch
Finish: Meltonian Shoe Cream

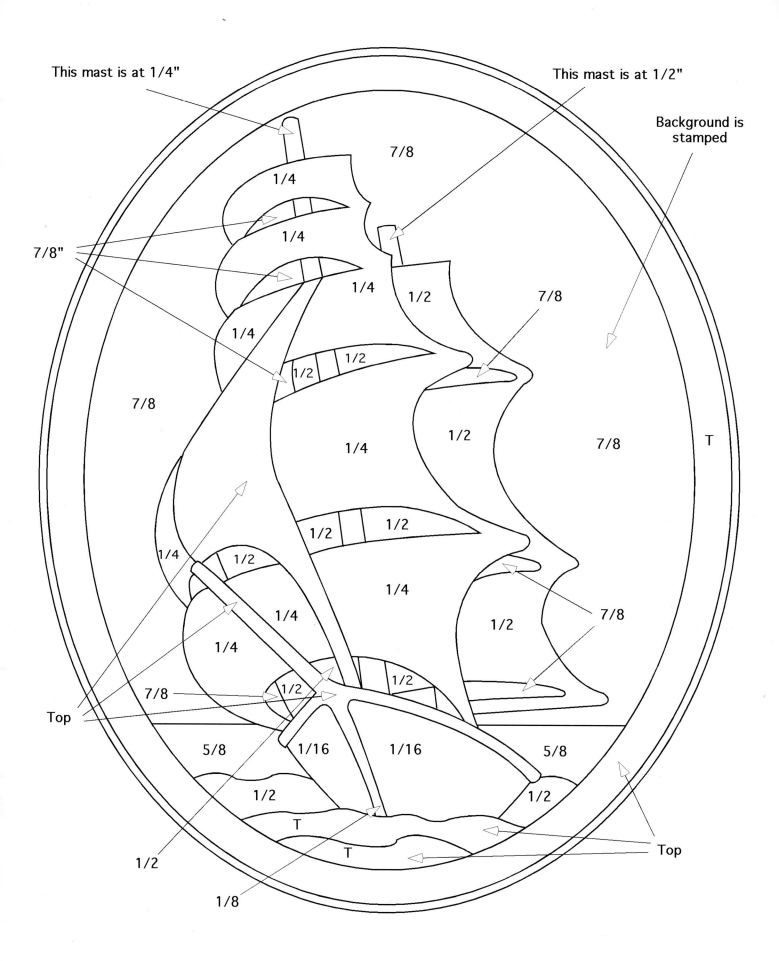

This mast is at 1/4"

This mast is at 1/2"

Background is
stamped

7/8

1/4

1/4

7/8"

1/4

1/4

1/4

1/2

7/8

1/2

7/8

1/2

1/2

7/8

1/4

1/2

7/8

1/4

1/2

1/2

1/2

1/4

1/4

1/4

7/8

1/4

1/4

1/2

1/2

Top

5/8

1/16

1/16

5/8

7/8

1/2

1/2

Top

1/2

T

1/2

T

1/8

T

14

About this Pattern

This pattern is a small project intended for carvers who want to try relief carving for the first time after having first sampled other types of carving.

I use this pattern regularly in my carving classes and at seminars as an instructional piece, because it allows me to demonstrate the technique of layering design components to achieve perspective. It will allow you to experiment with toolmarking large surfaces to achieve consistent texture, which is not all that easy at first. Several basic hand skills need to be mastered before the sails look even and full and the carving attains sharp definition and clean lines.

This is an easy panel to assemble, and can be made of two boards, like the finished sample by one of my advanced students, Hans Dietrich. He used 2" thick Alberta white birch for this piece, one of the finest relief carving woods in the world.

Hans is a "clean" carver whose steady hands never fail to produce pleasing carvings. He decided to finish this piece with wax-based cream-stain (ssshhh! It's shoe cream!) in order to enhance the toolmarking and soften the appearance of the wood. This finish is applied with a tooth brush, brushed out with a shoe brush and then buffed with a soft cloth in a one-step process.

There was no sanding at all in this carving. Sanding is the "S" word in my carving studio and is not permitted unless the student is willing to put up with jokes and friendly ribbing for a week or so. The smooth appearance of the carving pictured here is the result of crisp, tidy toolmarking with razor sharp tools.

The Panel

To use this pattern, you must first enlarge it to 12" by $14\frac{1}{2}$" using a photocopier, a pantograph or a grid system. This will make it roughly a 150% enlargement. The panel should be constructed using 2" thick wood, so it is no smaller than 13" by $15\frac{1}{2}$", to allow you to place the pattern in the most advantageous position on the panel.

As mentioned elsewhere, please do not try to get away without laminating at least two boards to form this panel. A single board is too unstable, and will warp and twist as you carve it. A laminated board will resist the tendency to distort.

Transfer the pattern to the prepared panel using carbon paper, and you will be ready to start carving.

Carving Hints

Start by routering the $\frac{7}{8}$" level, and work your way up to the $\frac{1}{16}$" level. Remove the waste wood at each level, from lowest to highest. This will unfortunately result in the loss of most of your pattern lines. Only the lines surrounding the top levels will remain.

If you carve the top areas to their lines, you will be able to accurately place the lines on the next lower level by cutting the top levels out of your pattern, laying the remaining parts of the pattern on the wood and re-tracing the lines using carbon paper. It is hard to "eye-ball" the lines in this pattern. Try to be as accurate as possible.

When each layer is carved to its lines, then you are ready to model the ship and the water.

Much of the ship is quite flat, with rounding occurring at the left edges of the sails and the bow. The foremost sail is mostly flat except where it gently slopes downward to the mast at the top and to the rail at the bottom. The second and third layers of sails should be rounded only on their left edges. The center portion and right edges are basically flat.

The heaviest texturing is left to the waves, where a #8-7mm gouge can be used. The sails and the masts require tooling with a #3-5mm gouge, every toolmark overlapping the adjoining toolmarks.

Stamping is applied to the background to create a contrast between the foreground and background elements. Stamped areas do not reflect light and so appear darker. The additional benefit to stamping lines is the fact that they cover up all the stray tool cuts on the background. I like to say that stamping "covers a multitude of (carving) sins."

The sails must be undercut if the ship is to appear to be raised off the background. In addition, all the edges of the sails, rails and panel edges need to be softened with bevels. Otherwise the edges will look rough and harsh, and the carving will lack definition.

Remember to observe closely which of the tight little spaces in this pattern belong to the background (the stamped areas) and which belong to the middle and background sails. A mistake here will be hard to repair.

The masts are rounded off on their edges, but only a little, otherwise they will look strange.

Be sure to toolmark the outside border of the panel and to carve your name somewhere on the outside of the oval containing the ship.

The flag in the photo is left off the pattern for a reason: It is very fragile, and few manage to carve it without breaking it one or two times. Perhaps you will want to take the risk, but don't feel that the carving is any less successful without it. You will have to guess if Hans managed to carve the flag without breaking it.

The $1/2$" wide ring around the ship is also optional, although the carving will look a little bit austere without it. The ring is rounded slightly, requiring a v-groove on its outside edge to accommodate the rounding.

Finally, apply a $1/8$" wide bevel to the outside edge of the carving to make it soft to the touch and to visually clean up the edge. You're done!

The Prospector

Artist: Hans Dietrich
Dimensions: 14" by 18"
Wood: Silver Maple
Finish: Meltonian Shoe Cream

About this Pattern

This carving has "cute and cuddly" written all over it: a weather-worn prospector with his little puppy friend, smiling for the camera. Like many others, I too am a sucker for "cute and cuddly."

Hans Dietrich did the carving in the photo, rendering the pattern beautifully. His carving is meticulously clean with not a single loose fiber of wood anywhere.

The features on the man's face are exaggerated with deep creases to make them more visible from a distance. The pupils in the eyes on both the man and his puppy are carved in classical fashion, hollowed out, rather than outlined. This makes the eyes appear to follow the viewer, adding a pleasant hint of realism.

Preferring to stain the completed work, Hans chose a cream-wax finish (ie: shoe cream) for his final finish. The color is similar to brown sugar. The advantage of staining is the way it brings out the toolmarking and evens the color across the panel. Since cream-wax stains are not liquid, they do not soak into the wood. Adhering only to the surface, they produce a consistent, pleasing finish of slightly less than satin sheen.

This pattern crops the prospector and puppy at chest level, and presents the two figures in a cameo-like setting. This is a favorite style of presentation in my carving classes because of its attractiveness, economy (no wasted space in the corners) and efficiency (takes less time to carve). The textures used on face, clothing, fur and hair are different from each other, making them easy to distinguish. To this range of textures were added the radial toolmarking immediately behind the two figures and the stamping on the outside border. The radial toolmarking leads the eye to the center of the carving where the figures lie, while the stamping on the boarder is meant to gather as little attention as possible.

The Panel

The original carving was 14" by 18", so this pattern needs to be enlarged by 200% if you wish it to be close to the original size. Use a photocopier or a pantograph to do the enlarging.

Choose wood that is of even grain and color, and laminate the panel with the boards oriented vertically. This carving is in 2" white birch, a favorite in our carving classes, but any other close-grained, light-colored wood will do, good examples being basswood, cherry, maple (hard, soft or silver) or even alder.

Avoid course-grained woods like oak, ash and butternut. They will likely not hold the detail, and if they do, the grain will compete with the relief for visibility. Avoid woods with a pronounced figure, that is, with a lot of variation in grain color or with dark heartwoods intruding into the lighter sapwood areas. These will destroy the beauty of the carving.

The finish of cream-wax is applied with a clean toothbrush, then buffed first with a clean bristle shoe-brush, followed by a soft flannel cloth. Don't use a shoe brush for the carving that was used previously to buff shoes. It may contain residues of a darker shoe cream color and ruin your finish. Be generous with the shoe cream so that each area receives as much stain as it can accept. The excess can be spread to an adjoining area and later removed with the buffing brush. If you apply too little to any one spot on the carving, you will end up with a blotchy, uneven appearance that will disappoint you. Because shoe cream is wax based, it resists any other finish applied later on making it impossible to re-apply another coat of cream-wax after the first has dried. Get it right the first time.

Carving Hints

After the pattern has been traced onto the panel using carbon paper, proceed to router the background to $1\frac{1}{8}$" on the outside border and $1\frac{1}{8}$" on the inside, leaving a small area between the dashed line and the inner edge of the interior border for a concave slope, as indicated by the pattern.

When the routering is complete, proceed to carve the pattern up to the lines, taking care not to leave any stop cuts in the background behind the figures.

Set the depths for the figures by hand, because they are shallow to begin with and less efficient to apply with a router. If you study the photo carefully, you will be able to tell by the shadows which areas are deeper that the others.

Here are a few clues: The man's hair, directly above the forehead, is the same height (top) as the tip of the nose and the high point of the mustache. His eyeballs are $1/4$" below top level, with the eyelids and cheeks occupying the layers between $1/4$" and top.

Similarly on the puppy, the high points of the nose, eyebrows and tongue are at top level. The tips of the ears are at $1/4$". Much of the leftmost paw is at top level too, while the rightmost paw is just $1/16$" lower at its highest point.

The deepest part of the man's face is between each eye and the bridge of the nose, where the relief drops to $3/8$", creating darker shadows than anywhere else, except the mouth.

The hair on the puppy is made with a #12-3mm v-tool. But then, so is the hair on the prospector. The difference is depth of cut. The puppy's hair is cut shallow, producing narrow grooves, and the old man's hair is cut much deeper, with coarser results.

Note how the v-toolmarks on the puppy go over the edge and even into the undercut area in some cases. Same for the prospector. Also notice how the ragged edges of the hairline add to the realistic appearance of the hair. Use a #12-6mm or #12-8mm v-tool to cut these notches. The bottoms and the shirt lines are also carved with a small v-tool.

The face, tongue, shirt and jacket are all toolmarked with a #3-5mm gouge to produce an even texture over these surfaces. Overlap your toolmarks so no original surface is left.

The radial toolmarking behind the two figures is made with a #12-3mm veiner. Aim these toolmarks to the center of the tip of the man's nose, and make sure you overlap your toolmarks thoroughly.

The interior border is toolmarked with a #2-16mm gouge so that it is nice and flat, while the exterior border is stamped. The outside edge of the carving is toolmarked the same as the interior border, and bevels are applied on the sharp edges of the two borders to soften their appearance and clean them up.

Finally, check your carving in a strong cross light, preferably natural light, at all angles to confirm that the carving is tidy. Then you are ready to apply the stain, if you wish, or a clear finish.

Ascending Lord

Artist: W.F. (Bill) Judt
Dimensions: 14" by 19 1/4"
Wood: White Birch
Finish: Clear Sanding Sealer

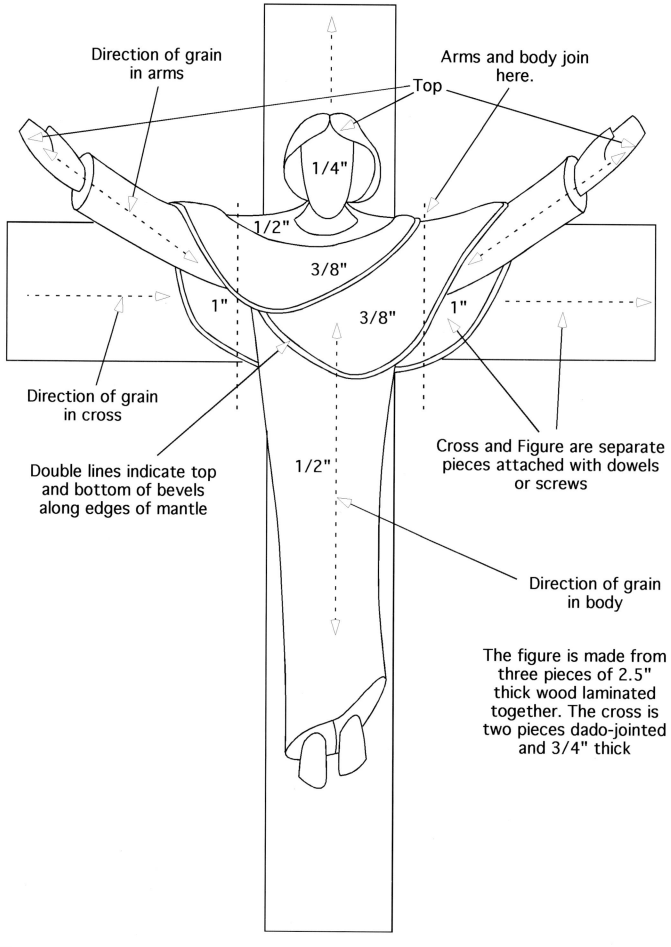

Direction of grain
in arms

Arms and body join
here.

Top

1/4"

1/2"

3/8"

1"

3/8"

1"

Direction of grain
in cross

Double lines indicate top
and bottom of bevels
along edges of mantle

1/2"

Cross and Figure are separate
pieces attached with dowels
or screws

Direction of grain
in body

The figure is made from
three pieces of 2.5"
thick wood laminated
together. The cross is
two pieces dado-jointed
and 3/4" thick

About this pattern

This pattern of the ascending Lord is one of my favorites, having used it for many years. This carving has found its way into numerous Christian schools, churches and private homes across Canada.

In contrast to the crucifix, which has been the dominant depiction of the image of Christ within the Christian community, this pattern is uplifting and joyful, and has been well received by those who wish an alternative to the rather solemn image of Christ crucified.

Whereas the crucifix rightly points to the power of Christ over sin, the image of the ascending Lord points to the power of Christ over the grave, and represents an Easter rather than a Good Friday focus. Thus it can be used to direct the believers' attention elsewhere than the suffering of their Lord.

The arms and hands are lifted above the cross, and the mantle of the garment drapes gently over the shoulder. Along with the face, hands, feet and hair, these components are rendered in a stylized fashion so that detail is reduced to the bare minimum.

Of the patterns in this book, this pattern is the most difficult to laminate, but one of the simplest to carve. The heavily undercut figure is toolmarked or scraped smooth so that the surfaces are simple and clean in appearance.

The cross and the figure are two separate pieces, attached at the back with screws or dowels. The figure is placed over the cross so it almost entirely covers the joints of the cross.

The cross is made of two pieces joined together with a dado joint. There is no carving needed on the cross, although I could easily imagine some chip carving providing it with delicate ornamentation.

The idea of this carving is to keep the figure as simple and stylized as possible, without making it difficult for the viewer to instantly recognize it as the ascending Lord.

The Panel

Laminate the cross first, using $3/4$" thick wood that is clear of knots and even in color. This select wood will make the work of constructing the cross easier, and the result will be a cross free of vibrant grain and bold knots that do not compete with the figure that will soon be placed on top of it. The finished size of the cross will be 14" by $19^1/_4$", which represents roughly a 200% enlargement of the pattern. Larger or smaller scaling is allowable, depending on your needs. The finished size of the figure itself will be $14^1/_2$" by $13^1/_2$", again representing a 200% enlargement of the pattern.

Carving Hints

Select clear, evenly colored wood for the body as well. The finished thickness should be $2^1/_2$". Prepare two pieces of this wood, one long enough to accommodate the main body of the pattern, and the other long enough for the two arms. Trace the pattern parts onto the wood with carbon paper.

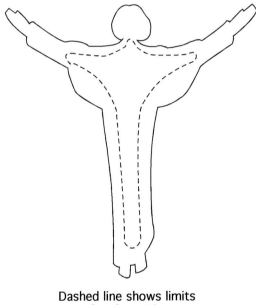

Dashed line shows limits
of undercutting

The arms must be oriented so the grain runs along the length of the arm rather than across it. This is for strength. Refer to the pattern for the correct orientation of the grain in relation to the arms and body.

The joint between the arms and the body must be tight and precise. There should be enough angle on the base of the arm to allow for the use of a jointer to assist you in preparing the mating surfaces. If you do not have a jointer, use a radial arm saw, a table saw or a miter saw to get the accurate cut, and then use a stationary sander to finish the joint surface.

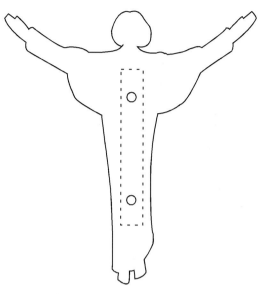

Block of wood is attached to the back to help you clamp the carving in a vise

Note that you must allow enough wood for the clamps in order to glue the arms, one at a time to the body. See the illustration to locate and orient these clamping surfaces.

A bandsaw is required to cut away the waste wood around the figure. Cut the arms out first, allowing additional wood for clamping blocks. Then cut the figure out as well. Bandsaw both the figure and the arms to the pencil line, but leave the line on the wood. This way your pattern is not cut away.

When the figure body and the arms are bandsawed (you did leave enough wood for the clamps to hold on to, didn't you?), proceed to glue and clamp the arms to the figure. I use a pipe clamp on this joint, along with an additional C-clamp to align the two pieces. Let the glue dry two hours before attaching the second arm, and overnight before you start working with the figure.

After the band sawing is complete, screw a $1^1/_2$" by $1^1/_2$" by 8" block of wood to the back of the assembled figure to allow you to clamp it securely in a vise for carving. Later, the block will be removed and the screw holes hidden by the cross.

The arms slope down to meet the body, which is lower than the arms and face. The intention here is to raise the arms and hands above the cross and toward the viewer. The hands are the highest point in the relief. The cross is made separately from two pieces of wood, dadoed and glued together.

Use whatever tools you have at hand to rough out the carving. As the carving approaches its final shape move to flatter tools—#2-16mm and #2-20mm are good—to smooth the surfaces in preparation for scraping. A scraper allows you to achieve a very smooth, consistent surface where the grain of the wood clearly shows through.

Bevels are applied to the edges of the cape to strengthen these edges, but also to help define the carving more clearly. Without these bevels, the carving will suffer.

Strive for clean, smooth surfaces with the minimum of noticeable toolmarking. This will produce a serene demeanor and bright reflective surfaces that will enhance the appearance of the figure.

Attach the figure to the cross from the back with screws set into pre-drilled and countersunk holes, and finish both the cross and the figure with a base coat of sanding sealer and a top coat of wax, according to the SSW method described in the beginning of this book.

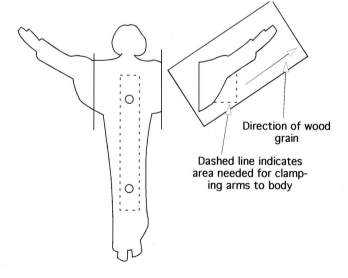

Direction of wood grain

Dashed line indicates area needed for clamping arms to body

Dall's Sheep

Artist: W.F. (Bill) Judt
Dimensions: 17" by 20"
Wood: White Birch
Finish: Meltonian Shoe Cream: Chamois

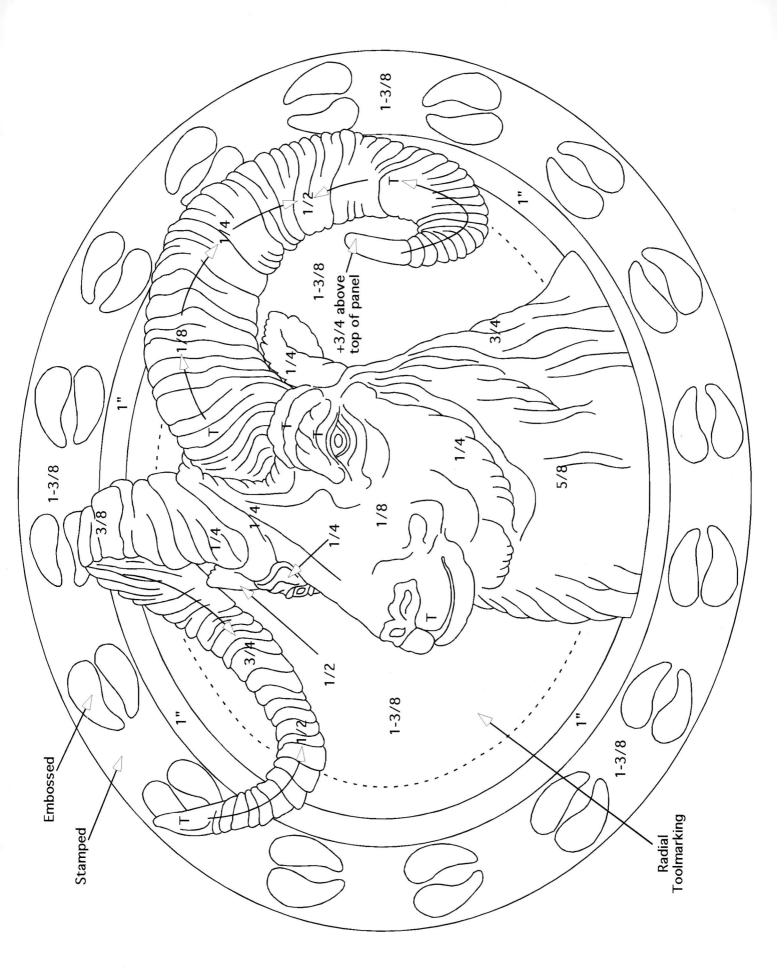

Embossed

Stamped

Radial
Toolmarking

26

About this Pattern

The "Dall's Sheep" is very challenging, even for the advanced carver. It was included in this treasury so that you can see what is possible with relief if one is careful with the use of depth compression and meticulous with directional toolmarking. Along with this, the Dall's sheep is a beautiful creature in a rugged sort of way and awesome in its ability to scale the heights of mountains with what appears to us as careless abandon. It has this way of looking sideways that makes those who are subject to its gaze think they are inferior. Tourists from around the world visit the Canadian Rockies for a glimpse of animals such as these and are rarely disappointed because the animals know they can intrude in human territory and quickly retreat to their own without the fear of humans following.

Among the patterns in the book, this one is unique in that it is carved in more than 2" of wood. A small piece of wood has been glued on top of the panel to allow the foreground horn to rise $3/4$" above the main panel, making the total panel thickness $2^3/4$". The cameo format enhances the appearance of depth and allows the horns to reach out over the recessed border.

Another interesting feature is the use of embossing to render the hoof prints on the stamped border. The highest point of each hoof print is the same height as the border area that surrounds it, except that the stamping drops slightly as it approaches the prints, making them appear higher. If you think of how quilting works, you will understand what is happening here.

Most of the face is carved in less than $1/4$" depth. Here it is important to accentuate what little actual relief exists with directional toolmarking, leading the eye of the viewer to assume shape and form. Most of the facial features move between the depths indicated on the pattern. You will have to study the photo to understand how surfaces slope and curve into one another.

The horns have slope indicators on them.

These arrows will help you understand how to model the horns in preparation for detailing. Keep in mind that even when properly modeled, the horns will not look realistic until the final undercutting, detailing and texturing are applied.

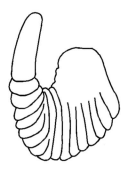

Horn Detail

This is the section of horn that must be added to the panel. Use 3/4" wood, and orient the grain the same direction as the underlying wood. Ensure that the same color wood is used.

It should be relatively easy for you to duplicate the fur, as the photo clearly shows the high points and low points and the direction of the tooling. Remember that there are very few straight lines in the fur, if any. Most are some variation of the classic S-curve. The S-curve allows you to move from one area over a slope into the adjoining area easily. The S-curve also allows you to disguise a flat area so it appears either rippled with muscle or covered with thick fur.

The eyes of the sheep are not round. They are more football shaped, with the length of the eye parallel to horizontal. The pupils here have been rendered with the classic hollow shape.

The Panel

The finished carving is about 17" by 20", which is approximately a 200% to 220% enlargement of this pattern. Choose wood that is even grained and consistent in color and figure, placing the sapwood to the front, and laminating so the boards are oriented vertically. Building some camber into the panel will help to control the tendency of the panel to cup to the carved side. Use stock that is a full 2" thick. To that you will add a $3/4$" thick piece of wood for the foreground horn. However, you must router the main panel *before* you add the extra piece for the horn.

This carving uses more depth than any of the others, moving down to $1^3/_8$" from the top of the main panel. Add to this the $^3/_4$" for the foreground horn, and this relief uses all of $2^1/_8$" of depth.

This carving is done in white birch, and has been stained with a cream wax finish (shoe cream). Avoid shoe waxes, because these contain far less pigment than the creams and are harder to apply. A clear finish using sanding sealer according to the SSW method is also perfectly acceptable.

The best overall place to hang this carving is where light crosses it from either side.

Carving Hints

When you start modeling the figure, pay attention to the sloped areas on the face, forehead, eyebrows and neck. These slopes vary constantly, requiring you to refer to the photo often. There are very few areas separated by stop cuts. Most areas blend smoothly into adjoining areas that are similarly toolmarked. Do not attempt to texture the fur on the sheep until the underlying body is shaped properly.

Undercutting will add a lot to the appearance of the sheep, especially in the area of the horns. Make sure the undercut is concave in shape rather than convex, as is so often the case with novice carvings. Concave undercuts are more convincing, and are accomplished by raising the handle of the tool as it moves toward the background. Convex undercuts happen when the handle is lowered while undercutting takes place. Try this out on a scrap to see how this works.

Some of the edges within the figure are also undercut. For example, the background horn, where it curls above the leftmost ear, the chin where it overlaps the neck, the left side of the nose where it passes over the leftmost eye and finally, the inside of the rightmost ear.

The only bevels in this carving are those along the eyelids, along the edges of the interior border, along the edge of the outside border and at the base of the sheep's neck. The rest of the edges are rounded over.

The fur is tooled with a #12-3mm v-tool, with vertical notches along the edges of the ears to make it look lifelike. The fur must be carved over the edge of the animal's body and face so that it actually moves into the undercut area slightly. This makes the perimeter of the animal look realistic by texturing what would otherwise be a smooth perimeter.

The horns are toolmarked across their width rather than along their length. This accentuates their shape. Use a variety of gouges for this texturing, including a #3-5mm, a #5-5mm and a #5-3mm. V-tools will help to make the grooves between sections of the horns. Be sure to carve over the edge of the horns so their perimeters look clean and realistic.

With the panel in an end vise, use a #2-20mm gouge to toolmark the outside edge of the carving, removing all evidence of the bandsaw. Then apply a light bevel to the corner of the outside edge.

Finish the carving with a clear sealer according to the SSW method or stain it with a cream wax, but don't choose a color that is too dark.

Eagle Landscape

Artist: Dennis McIntosh
Dimensions: 20" diameter
Wood: White Birch
Finish: Clear Sanding Sealer

About this Pattern

Eagles have long been a favorite subject for artists, and no less among the students in my carving classes, where it seems hardly a course goes by without at least one carver working on an eagle.

This carving was done by Dennis McIntosh, a happily retired fellow who took up carving as a hobby a few short years ago. As you can see by the photo, Dennis has not taken long to master the essentials of relief carving, and to move on to the more advanced techniques. He decided to invest extra time on the eagle, adding texture to each feather instead of carving them smooth. This has added a level of realism to the carving that is quite pleasant to behold. His work is tidy, balanced and carefully executed.

Careful layering of design elements is necessary to achieve convincing perspective in any relief, but more so in a relief landscape such as this. It is just as important to use a variety of textures to distinguish one layer of the relief from another.

The eagle looks to have caught a wind current in its strong wings. This effect is achieved by orienting the bird at a slightly upward angle, and orienting the clouds so they appear to rise from left to right, having also been lifted by the wind. The underside of the bird's wing comprises concave surfaces that must be accurately modeled if they are to look realistic. Then the feathers can be re-drawn and carved.

The cameo method of presentation is also employed in this pattern. The figures are raised above a background of a different texture and tone. Undercutting is used to enhance the cameo effect, along with stamping in the background. The exterior, which is the lowest point in the carving plays a supporting role without acting as a container for the pattern. This border is also tool-marked in a radial pattern so that the viewer's eye is led to the interior of the carving where the eagle is displayed.

The foreground trees are merely silhouettes

with vertical texturing, but they curve downward as they approach the center of the carving. This adds some interest to what could otherwise be a flat, boring tree line. The top edge of each tree line is slightly beveled to take away the sharp edges and make the perimeter visible from the front.

Bevels are utilized along the edges of the feathers throughout the carving. These bevels are crucial if the feathers are to be well defined. They turn an otherwise vertical edge forward, from perpendicular to the surface (90°) to between 60° and 45° to the surface. The drawing below illustrates the proper use of bevels on the feathers.

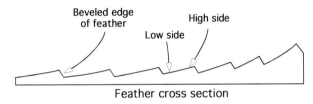

Feather cross section

The clouds, also, are mere silhouettes, rounded on the edges and toolmarked evenly with a short, bold stroke. They need no more detail than that to serve as embellishments to the design.

The Panel

The finished carving is about 20" in diameter, which is approximately a 270% enlargement of this pattern. If you prefer a smaller panel, a 200% enlargement of the pattern will do nicely. Choose wood that is even grained and consistent in color and figure. Then laminate a panel that is one inch wider and longer than the pattern to allow extra room for placing the pattern in the best spot. Remove all knots and defects from the wood before preparing it for lamination. Defects will ruin this carving.

Place the sapwood to the front, and laminate so the boards are oriented vertically. Try to build some camber into the panel to help control the tendency of the panel to cup to the carved side. Use 2" thick stock.

White birch was used for this carving, but any close-grained wood, especially those that are light in color, will be suitable. The grain of coarser woods will make it difficult to carve the finer detail and will compete with the relief for visibility.

Choose a clear, satin finish for the finished carving. Staining this piece is an acceptable alternative, but stick with the earth-tone colors. Use a wax-based stain like shoe cream.

The best overall place to hang this carving is where light crosses it from either side. This will cast shadow across the bevels, allowing the viewer to see the relief. The bevels do most of the work in presenting this eagle to the viewer.

Carving Hints

After the pattern is transferred to the panel using carbon paper, bandsaw the panel to size. Then use a router to set the depths according to the pattern. Rough out the carving to the lines.

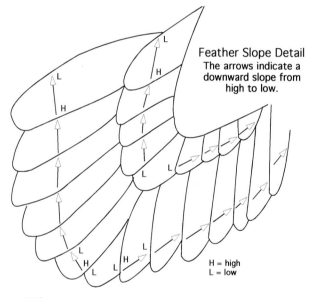

Feather Slope Detail
The arrows indicate a downward slope from high to low.

H = high
L = low

When you start modeling the figures, pay attention to the sloped areas on the wings. These slopes must be carved by hand according to the direction of the arrows, which point from the high to the low point. Then the wings must be smoothly modeled in order to make it easier to redraw the feathers.

Once the feathers are redrawn, they may be carved. I start with a small v-tool, say a #12-3mm, cutting a shallow groove along the low (L = low)

side of the line on each feather. The feathers are then stop-cut precisely to shape, and the slopes are created with a shallow #3-12mm tool, or perhaps a narrow skew in the corners.

The beak is smooth, except for the various grooves and v-cuts that define its features. The pupil in the eye is hollow. The eagle's hood is tool-marked with a #11-3mm veiner. Observe the photo to see the direction of the veiner cuts.

The legs are tooled with a #12-3mm v-tool and notched along their edges to make them look life-like. The body of the eagle is tooled with a #5-8mm gouge, making sure that the toolmarks overlap each other thoroughly.

Toolmark the foreground tree layer with a #5-5mm gouge and the deeper tree layer with a #11-3mm veiner. Keep these toolmarks relatively, but not strictly, vertical. The clouds are tooled horizontally with a #7-10mm gouge, ensuring that the toolmarks follow over the edge of the clouds till they meet the stamped background. This makes for a more attractive edge to the clouds.

Undercutting helps to enhance the roundness of the eagle and to add visual depth to the carving. Undercut all the figures carefully and in a tidy fashion, taking care to proceed carefully around the feathers to minimize breakage.

The edge of the stamped area has a large bevel applied to it, to help separate it from the border. When applying the radial toolmarking to the border, be sure to aim toward the exact center of the carving with each stroke. This will make the pattern of strokes look consistent and true. A bevel is also needed on the edge of each tree level. No bevels are applied on the clouds, as they are rounded over and toolmarked instead.

With the panel in an end vise, use a #2-20mm gouge to toolmark the outside edge of the carving, removing all evidence of the bandsaw. Then apply a light bevel to the corner of the outside edge.

Finish the carving with a clear sealer according to the SSW method, add hangers to the back, and hang it on the wall. You are done!

Father and Child

Artist: Ron Bush
Dimensions: 15 by 13¼"
Wood: White Birch
Finish: Clear Sanding Sealer

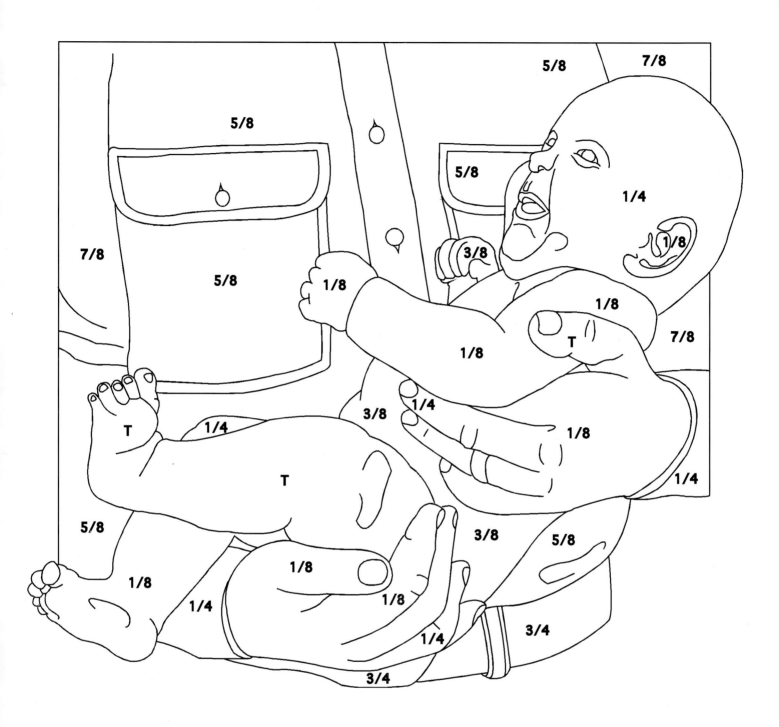

About this Pattern

Here is a pattern that appeals to almost everyone. A father tenderly holds his little child in his arms, eliciting a smile of pleasure on the face of his little one. Boy or girl? If you can't tell, then I won't tell either. <grin>

This splendid piece was carved by Ron Bush, one of the "lifers" in my carving class. At the time this book was published, Ron had taken every course I have offered for eleven years straight, with no sign to indicate this will not continue for the foreseeable future. Part of it, I think, is that he really likes the people he meets in carving class, but the greatest part is that he loves carving. And he is good at it too, always coming up with new ideas and challenges that keep his instructor on his toes.

Ron is a welder/millwright for a local forestry company, and a talented one at that, who is respected by his co-workers for his quality work. His desire to achieve a high standard of workmanship is reflected in all his carvings, including this one.

I like the casual look the father has, with his buttoned pockets, flannel work shirt and thick belt holding up what must be denim jeans. I also like the way the child displays his happiness, with a toothless smile, fists scrunched tight, toes wriggling and legs kicking. You can almost feel the smooth skin and smell its fresh-bathed fragrance.

This carving has no borders and little background except the shape of the father. His shape is cropped so that only what is essential remains, just enough to let us know he is the child's father. The baby, on the other hand, is shown completely, and even hangs over the edge of the picture. This method of judicious cropping places the focus on the child, and places the father in a supporting role, thus mimicking what happens in real life.

The Panel

Enlarge this pattern 200% using a photocopier or a pantograph.

This is one of the smaller carvings in this treasury, measuring only 15" wide by $13^{1}/_{4}$" tall by 2" thick. It was carved in beautiful white birch that was knot and heartwood-free. It was finished with a basecoat of clear quick-drying sanding sealer and a topcoat of paste wax. The laminations are horizontal, although vertical laminations will also work on this small panel. As a rule, laminations need to be parallel to the longest axis in a panel in order to minimize cupping. But in this case, the vertical and horizontal axes are close enough that it won't matter. Be sure to use dry wood and add a little camber to the panel when you are laminating to help control the cupping of the wood.

This pattern needs a fine-grained wood to look the best. White birch, yellow birch, maple, cherry, basswood, even alder are suitable. Coarse grain in woods like oak, ash and butternut will compete with the relief for visibility, obscuring the details of the carving. Be sure that your wood has a subdued figure (consistent color and little contrast) and is clear of the darker-colored heartwood. Dramatic color changes across the carving will compete for the attention of the viewer to the distraction and detriment of the relief.

Because a large part of the carving is smooth skin, care must be taken to apply smooth, clean toolmarking on the father's hands and to the child's entire body. The smoother your toolmarking, the smoother the appearance of the skin. Sharp tools are an absolute necessity.

The father's shirt must be carved with equal care, but with small, noticeably concave gouge marks to simulate the texture of the flannel shirt.

Undercutting is also essential in order to give the body of the child and the father's arms an appearance of roundness and perspective. There is so much compression of the dimension of depth in this carving, as much as 15:1, that even little things you do to simulate the appearance of shape and form are important.

You can see that this carving has no stamping on it. This is not normally the case, as stamping is such a useful texture. But it was decided that none of the surfaces in this carving warranted this rough, unreflective texture, and so it was not used.

Carving Hints

When the pattern is traced on the prepared panel with carbon paper, you can bandsaw the perimeter of the carving and router the various areas to the depths indicated in the pattern. The fractions indicated on the pattern are router depths only, and represent the highest point in a particular area that will later be rounded, sloped and otherwise modeled.

When toolmarking the baby's skin and the father's hands, use a #2-12mm, or a #2-8mm gouge. Some of the more concave surfaces will require #3 or #5 or #7 gouges to accomplish the task. The father's shirt is toolmarked with a #5-5mm or a #8-4mm gouge, or something close that will leave the surface looking consistently textured with small, round-bottomed tool cuts. The shirt should look uniformly rougher than the skin.

Creases in the fingers and toes are carved with a #12-3mm v-tool, as are the lines that define the shirt pockets, belt loop, cuffs and button areas. Some of the creases will look better if you place a stop-cut at the bottom to catch a darker line of shadow.

Avoid sanding this carving to achieve a smooth appearance. Sanding dulls the reflective qualities of the wood and erodes the toolmarks. A sharp tool will leave a shiny, reflective surface that will make your carving look far better. If you overlap your toolmarks, you will achieve the appearance of smoothness without much trouble.

Undercutting around the baby's feet and head and around the father's lower hand is more difficult because of the depths involved. Be sure your undercut angle is not so great that your tools will be unable to reach far enough under to complete the cuts cleanly. The baby's head, on the right side, is undercut down to the border in order to make it look less bulky. You will not want the edge of the head to look thick even if the carving is viewed from the far right.

Finally, toolmark the edges of the carving with clean gouge marks from a #3-16mm tool and apply bevels to the outside edge of the background and to the outside edge of the father's shirt, wrist and belt.

Goalie

Artist: Bob Neufeld
Dimensions: 20 by 14"
Wood: White Birch
Finish: Clear Sanding Sealer

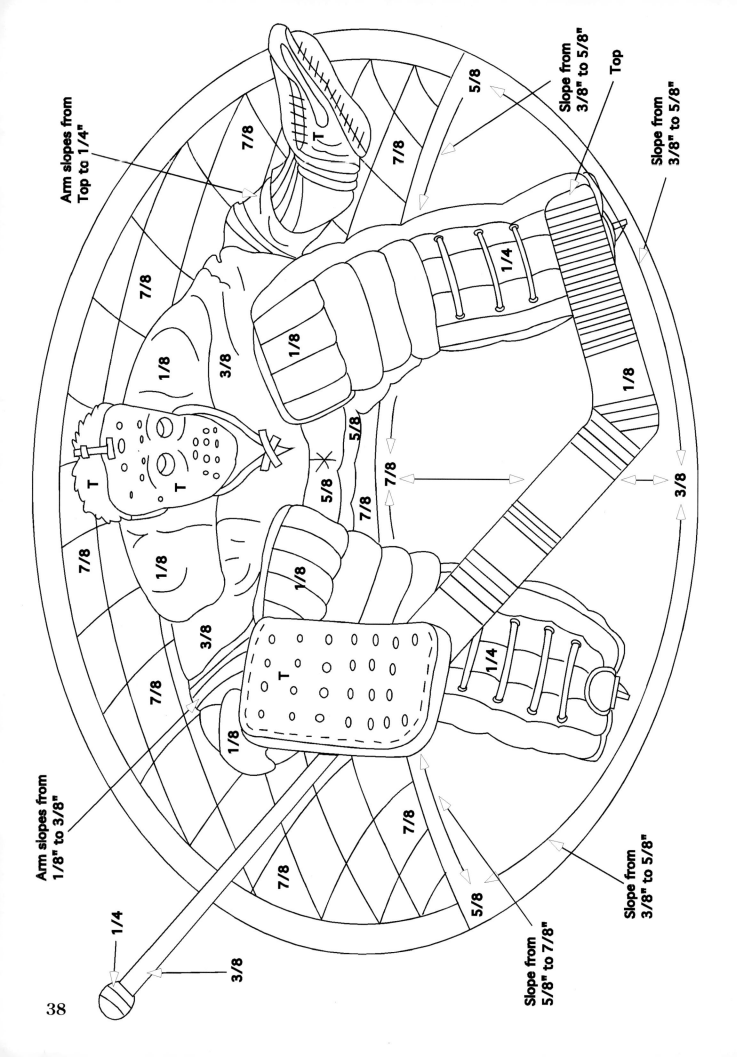

38

About this Pattern

When this pattern was in the process of being carved, my son, a minor league hockey goalie at the time, visited the carving class each week to monitor its progress. He was fascinated by it and had no trouble relating to the theme.

The fellow who carved and owns this little masterpiece is Bob Neufeld, a retired high school physical education teacher for whom hockey was the game of preference. Bob is also one of our "donut dudes," that is, one who brings donuts to class for us to enjoy with our coffee.

Bob has carved with me for almost ten years, as this book is being written, and is considered one on my "lifers." He is a spiritual man, an energetic outdoorsman and an ardent conservationist whose integrity and perseverance have earned him the respect of his peers. He is also a devoted family man and a proud grandfather.

Bob knew what he wanted this goalie to look like. His hair had to be matted with sweat, making him look frantic. His mask had to be glued to his face and droop slightly over his eyes. The pads had to look like bags of stuffing ready to burst but for the leather, stitching and straps that held them together. The stick had to be full size and layered with tape with a knob on the end, and the blocker and catcher had to be leather looking, because that's what they used when he played hockey years ago.

Bob and I struggled with the problem of how to include the net without carving it completely. The solution was to use netting as the texture for the background, allowing it to blend into the border, with the spaces stamped for contrast. To my mind it worked great.

The ice was easier to figure out, but a little harder to carve, because it required a steady slope from front center to each side, and from front center to mid-center. It also had to pass smoothly under the goalie as it made its way to the lower levels.

This pattern is an exciting challenge, because it allows for all sorts of detail to be added, and for the carver to improvise with textures.

Woodburning could also be used to enhance some of the details, like the stitching on the glove or the tape on the stick, or even to add skate marks on the ice.

The Panel

To use this design you will have to enlarge it to 20" wide by 14" tall, including the stick which protrudes outside the ellipse. Set the copier to 200% enlargement for best results.

Prepare a relief panel measuring 21" wide by 15" tall to accommodate the pattern, which can then be transferred on with carbon paper. Your panel should be constructed from two, three or four boards whose lengths are oriented horizontally for strength.

Use the depths indicated to establish the levels for each of the areas in the pattern. These depth indications are the high points from which you will start modeling each area of the carving. The arrows indicate areas where a gentle, smooth slope is needed. The slope should pass smoothly under the goalie as it moves steadily towards the netting.

The handle of the stick should be made from a separate piece of wood, cut so the grain runs lengthwise for strength. After the carving is roughed out, the stick can be fitted so that it slides under the blocker where it can then be glued onto the background (before the netting is carved) with a thick mixture of sawdust and wood glue. Clamp it overnight. Be sure to carve away all traces of excess glue so that your final finish is not marred.

Carving Hints

Shape the pads, blocker, glove and jersey so they don't look stiff and flat. It is wise to round their edges and hollow their surfaces before attempting to apply details like creases, holes and straps. Use a #9-5mm gouge to carve the curves and hollows on the jersey. Note that the pants sit lower than the jersey, but are carved the same way.

Goalie

After the modeling is complete, the goalie receives heavy undercutting along his entire perimeter to make him stand out from the background. Then the pads can be detailed so they appear heavily quilted, and the straps can be lowered below the surface of the pads to suggest they are straining to hold the pads in shape. Use a #12-3mm v-tool to help carve the creases and the straps. Now shape the stick and the handle so they slope gently downward from the heel of the stick to the knob at the end. This gentle slope should appear to pass evenly under the blocker.

After all modeling is completed, the entire figure needs to be toolmarked smoothly using #2 and #3 gouges in widths from 3mm to 12mm. Orient the toolmarks to accentuate the shape on the goalie, especially on the jersey.

The hair must be tooled with a #12-3mm v-tool, as must the tape lines on the stick and the laces on the jersey. Try to give the hair a "frantic" look. If the eyes are carved deep behind the mask, so they look up from under the top edge of the mask, they will enhance this frantic look.

The netting is carved first with a v-tool and then with a skew chisel, which is used to apply bevels to the edges. The surfaces between the netting must be quilted slightly before being stamped. Stamping gives the area between the netting a distinctive texture that will appear darker when finished.

The ice should be carved as smooth as possible, using a #2-12 or #2-16 gouge. Overlapped toolcuts will make the surface even flatter. If you want to put skate blade marks in the ice, use a #12-2mm v-tool to do this, but try it out on a scrap of wood first. Use a pencil to lightly draw where the skate marks will be cut.

A #11-3mm veiner will do a nice job of carving the small holes in the blocker and the mask, and a #11-2mm veiner will help you carve the holes into which the laces pass.

Finally, carve the perimeter of the carving smooth using a #3-20mm gouge, and apply a smooth bevel to the front and back edge of the perimeter to soften its appearance and make the carving more comfortable to hold.

The carving can now be finished using the SSW method. Add screws and wire to the back, and the job is done.

Howling Wolf

Artist: Laurette Cissel
Dimensions: 17½" by 24
Wood: White Birch
Finish: Clear Sanding Sealer

L.R. CISSEL

About this Pattern

On a cliff overlooking the night time forest, a lone wolf howls at the full moon while clouds lazily drift between the trees and the moon. Like sentinels, the trees reach for the sky as if to help the wolf lift his moon-song upwards.

This pattern will provide you with many hours of challenge and pleasant relaxation. Technically, it is not as difficult as some of the others in this book, but it will take some time to complete. Regardless, it is a delightful pattern and the finished carving will be a visual treat. We can thank Laurette Cissel for contributing her excellent carving for our photograph. This is a fine expression of her technical skill and her love of carving.

Take a moment to consider the following features of this pattern:

1. It does not use a border to constrain or restrict the design components.

2. The background plays a supporting role without interfering with the design components that lay on top of it.

3. The background is recessed on three sides to create the effect of an irregular border.

4. The trees lean outward, thereby leading the eye towards the wolf.

5. The wolf stands on the cliff which serves as a foreground for the carving.

6. The stamped background does not reflect light. Instead, it provides a contrast to the otherwise bright and reflective surfaces of the carving. This produces a visual effect similar to a photo negative.

7. The fur is v-tooled in a manner that accentuates the shape of the animal, helping to increase the appearance of depth and shape.

The Panel

The full size of this pattern is 17$\frac{1}{2}$" by 24", so you will have to enlarge this pattern roughly 240% to 250% using a photocopier or a pantograph. My preference is to use a pantograph so that I am left with a pencil line which can be more easily edited by hand. This way, even if I have an excellent pattern in front of me, I can still improve it or alter it to suit my needs.

Laminate the panel using 2" wood, white birch if possible, orienting the laminations vertically. Other woods that will work are those that have a subdued figure, are light in color and possess a close grain. Be sure to allow an extra inch on the width and height of the panel so you have room to place the complete pattern on the wood.

You will have to use a bandsaw to cut out the irregular perimeter of the pattern from the rectangular panel. Be careful doing this, that you don't accidentally remove some of the tree branches.

Observe how the rectangular background appears to pass under the tree branches and the tail of the wolf, which overhangs the edge. This effect is achieved through careful undercutting of the tail and trees as they move over the edge of the background. In fact, all the components of this pattern are neatly undercut to make them appear independent of the supporting background.

This carving is finished with a clear sanding sealer basecoat and a topcoat of clear paste wax, with a rubbing with clean steel wool between basecoat and top coat. Be especially sure to clean the carving thoroughly after using the steel wool. A vacuum helps to suck up the wool fibers.

Carving Hints

The stamping on the background should be dense, saturated and consistent if it is not to appear blotchy. Take time to stamp under every part that is undercut and into the tight spots.

The clouds are toolmarked using a #9-3mm gouge. Keep these tool cuts short, clean and horizontal. Even the edges of the clouds should be toolmarked with this tool.

The moon can be textured with a #2-16mm gouge. This shallow tool will leave the moon's surface quite flat and smooth. Be sure to gently round the moon's edges.

The tree trunks are textured with shallow toolmarks from a #11-3mm veiner. The toolmarks move about an inch in height at a diagonal across the tree, from bottom left to top right as they cross the trunk. This gives the trunk a realistic appearance, as bark generally moves in a spiral upwards around the tree trunk.

The tree boughs are tooled with a #12-6mm or #12-8mm v-tool. This v-tool is larger than the #12-3mm v-tool that is used to carve the fur on the wolf. The larger size allows a certain coarseness in the boughs, which appear quite distinct from the texture of the fur. Note how the v-tool is used vertically to notch the edges of each bough in order to create a rough, irregular effect. The grass on top of the cliff is textured vertically with the larger v-tool and notched along the top edge.

Use a #5-8mm gouge to toolmark the smooth surfaces of the cliff, orienting the toolmarks so they follow the ridges between sections of the cliff. Use a #8-7mm to toolmark the lower right foreground, orienting them horizontally.

Carving knots into the tree trunks and hollowing the ends of broken branches are especially nice touches. They make the branches come alive.

The eye, the nose, the lower lip and the teeth of the wolf can be carved smooth. To make the wolf's body especially realistic, be sure to carve the hollows in the legs where the tendons show, and the hollows between the hind leg and the chest, and the neck and the chest. There is also a hollow separating the jaw from the neck and very shallow hollows around the eye socket.

As usual, the outside edge of the carving, both on the underside of the parts that overhang and the edge of the supporting background, needs to be toolmarked with a #3-16mm gouge to remove all the original bandsaw marks. Finally, use a 16mm skew to bevel the sharp outside edges of the background, the dead tree trunk and the cliff.

Irises

Artist: Neil Dobson
Dimensions: 12½" by 16
Wood: White Birch
Finish: Clear Sanding Sealer

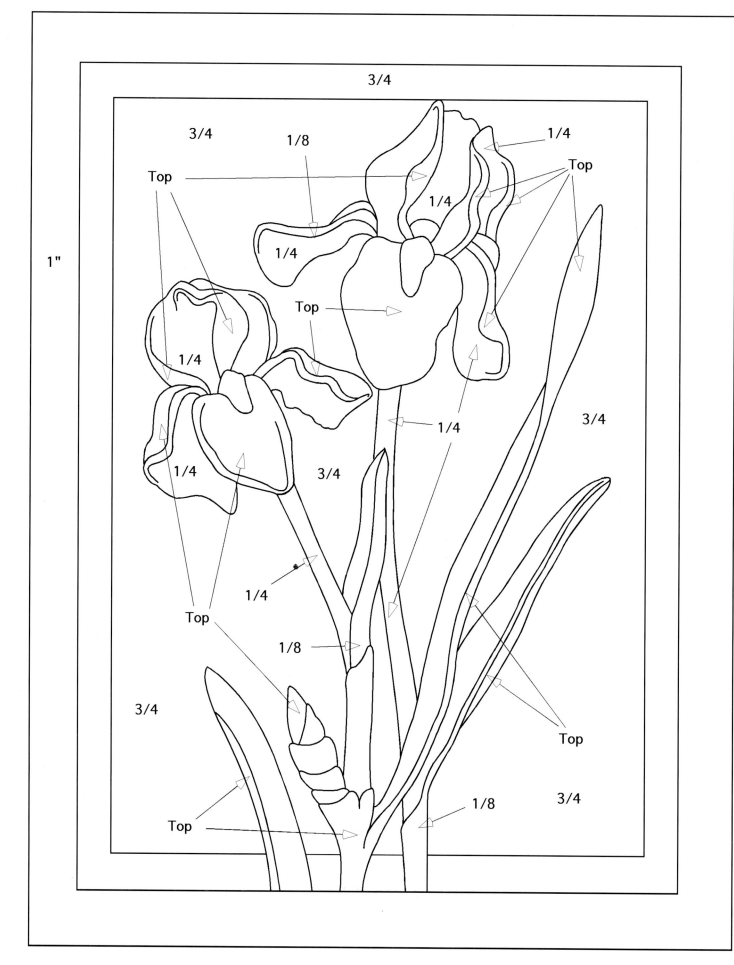

46

About this Pattern

The original idea for this pattern came from a stained glass design that was adapted using photos of real irises to add detail and realism. I use this carving as an instructional piece because it presents the student with many interesting challenges, most notable the problem of making sense of petals whose surfaces twist up and over and around.

What happens when you try to carve these petals is the same as what happens when you try to carve, for instance, the folds of a figure's flowing robe. Neither fabric or petals are flat, but instead present surfaces that twist, overlap and change plane constantly. There is an inside, an outside, a topside and an underside. There are edges and twists and undercutting. Quite challenging indeed.

Neil Dobson, who carved the example used in this book, managed to wrap his mind around the design quite successfully, in my opinion. Being a veteran school teacher has taught him that persistence and patience are useful tools when trying to understand patterns and children alike. In fact, he liked the design so much he carved it twice, making some changes to the border and background on the second carving just so it would be different. This pattern is a cameo, that is, the irises are raised above a background of a different color and texture. The smooth lines and bevels of the irises contrast with the stamped, non-reflective background in typical cameo fashion.

The base of the stems and leaves are neatly cropped at the edge of the interior border, which stands slightly raised above the outside border. The two borders are distinguished by different toolmarking. I like the way the outside border is toolmarked so that it looks like a mitered frame.

The stamped background is not entirely flat, but slopes down slightly at its perimeter as it approaches the interior border, giving it a quilted appearance. The stamping is consistent with no gaps or variation in density. It is important to apply stamping in this fashion to avoid drawing undue attention to the stamping to the detriment of the flowers, which should be the true focus of the carving. Uneven stamping is like a floor with a squeak in it, drawing attention to itself every time one passes over it.

Undercutting is another important feature of this carving. Without even and controlled undercutting, these irises would look thick and unnatural. Undercutting hides the sides of the flowers, leaves and stems from the viewer, giving them the appearance of being self-supporting and raised above the background.

Because the stems and leaves, in particular, are thin, it is easy to undercut to the point where you break through from one side of the leaf or stem to the other, weakening the part significantly. This you want to avoid.

The Panel

The original carving was 12$\frac{1}{2}$" by 16", so this pattern needs to be enlarged by 150-175% if you wish it to be close to the original size. Use a photocopier or a pantograph to do the enlarging.

Choose wood that is of even grain and color, and laminate the panel with the boards oriented vertically. This carving is done in 2" white birch, but any other close-grained, light-colored wood will do, good examples being basswood, cherry, maple (hard, soft or silver), or even alder.

Course-grained woods like oak, ash and butternut will also work as long as you are able to carve them comfortably. The grain will make it easier to see the subtle contours of the irises. This is not always the case with course-grained woods whose grain most often competes with the relief to the point where it is hard to see that caving for the grain. The stamped areas will subdue the course grain so that it is less visible and less in competition with the irises for attention.

Avoid woods with a pronounced figure, that is, with a lot of variation in grain color or with dark heartwoods intruding into the lighter sapwood areas. These will destroy the beauty of the carving.

Irises

Carving Hints

After the pattern has been traced onto the panel using carbon paper, proceed to router the background to 1" on the outside and 3/4" on the inside, according to the pattern. The depths indicated on the irises themselves will not be routered, those being more suited to handwork than to power tools.

When the routering is complete, proceed to carve the pattern up to the lines, taking care not to leave any stop cuts in the background along the base of the petals, leaves or stems. If you do, these cuts will be "orphaned," that is, they will remain separated from the edges when you undercut the irises, and will serve only to remind you that your stop-cutting was too vigorous.

The petals will be toolmarked with #3-8mm and #3-5mm gouges. The stems will be smoothed with a flatter tool, like an 8mm skew chisel, because the chisel smooths a convex surface better than a gouge. Tight areas under petals must be shaped with whatever tool will do the job.

When the petals and leaves are shaped and toolmarked you must apply bevels to their edges, in order to strengthen them and make them more visible to the viewer. Sharp edges are not easy to see, but beveled edges catch light or shadow that is visible from the front, enhancing the overall definition of the carving.

The drawing below shows more clearly the inside, outside and topside of the petals and leaves. Study this carefully, referring to the color photo for further clarification. The main pattern shows the relative depth of these various areas.

Keep in mind that these areas are not flat, but move smoothly from one depth to another. Stop cuts should only be used on an edge where one area overlaps another.

The outside edge of the carving is toolmarked with a #3-16mm gouge, overlapping each cut so as to carve away any trace of the original bandsaw marks. Bevels are applied to the edge of the outside border and the edge of the interior border.

This carving is finished clear, but an application of cream-wax stain (cream shoe polish applied with a tooth brush and buffed with a clean bristle brush and a soft cloth) will also work nicely. Just be sure to choose a color that is not too dark. I always sample the color on a small piece of smooth wood (the same type as will be used in the carving) before I buy the jar of shoe cream, just to be sure.

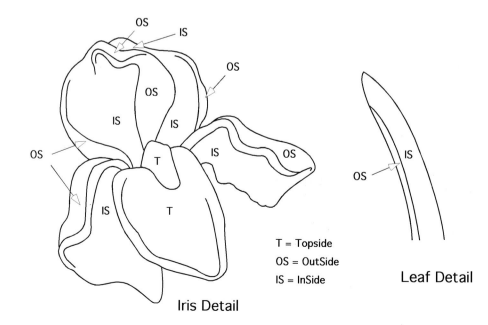

T = Topside
OS = OutSide
IS = InSide

Iris Detail

Leaf Detail

Come Unto Me

Artist: W.F. (Bill) Judt
Dimensions: 19" diameter
Wood: Red Oak
Finish: Clear Sanding Sealer

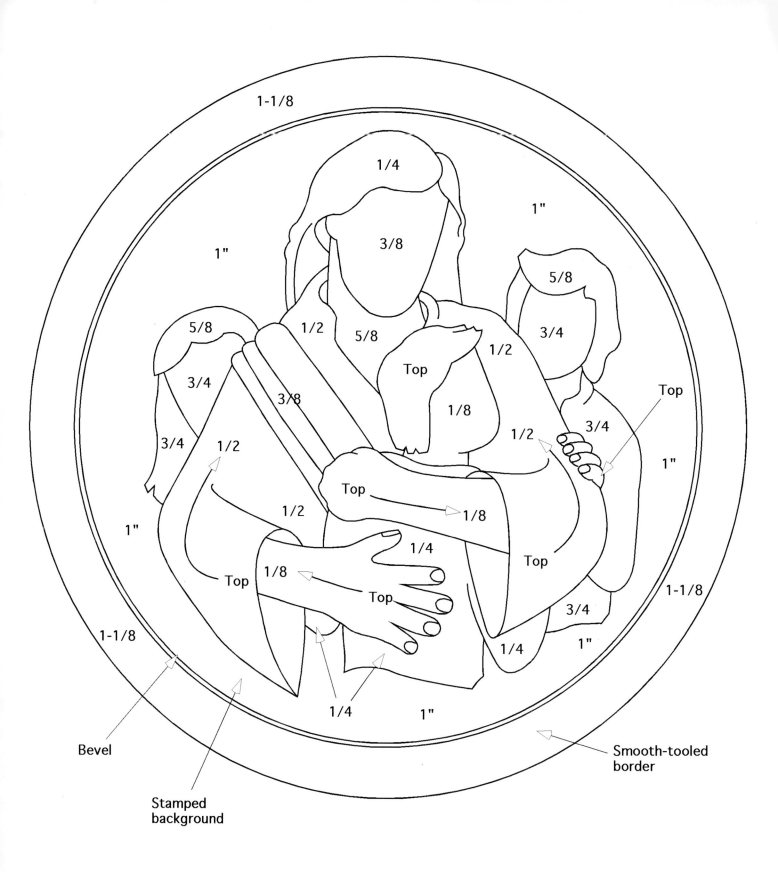

1-1/8

1/4

1"

1"

3/8

5/8

5/8

3/4

1/2

5/8

3/4

Top

3/8

1/2

1/8

3/4

Top

3/4

1/2

1/2

3/4

Top

3/4

Top

1/8

1"

1/2

Top

1/8

1/8

1/4

Top

Top

1/8

1-1/8

1-1/8

1/4

3/4

1"

Bevel

1/4

1"

1"

Smooth-tooled
border

Stamped
background

About this Pattern

This pattern was developed in my studio a number of years ago and has been used countless times in various forms. The original pattern was not as refined and balanced as the one in this book, but after having undergone many revisions this pattern is finally reaching a state of maturity.

I like this pattern for the way it conveys the gentleness of Jesus as he tenderly hugs a boy, with two other children looking on. The boy on the right has his hand on Jesus' arm, and the girl, who is a little younger, and perhaps a little more shy, is looking from the side to see what is happening.

This pattern, like many I carve, is based on a Biblical passage, specifically Luke 18:16, where Jesus uses the example of the children's faith to illustrate the faith required for discipleship. Because it illustrates one of the more familiar passages of sacred text, this carving will readily find a measure of acceptance in Christian churches and homes everywhere.

The absence of facial features is intentional. I wanted the figures to be reduced to their rudimentary form. To include features on the face would be to limit the effectiveness of these powerful symbols. The children are meant to represent every child, and figure of Jesus is meant to represent the concept of the "gentle Saviour."

Red oak was used in this carving so that its coarse grain would enhance the appearance of the simple figures, adding the suggestion of features to the face, and accentuating the contours of the hands, heads, arms and garments. The use of oak is successful in this carving because the shapes have been kept simple, and small detail has been avoided. Normally, the grain in oak is too powerful for relief carvings, overwhelming the detail and competing with the relief for visibility.

The cameo method of presentation is also employed in this pattern. The figures are raised above a background of a different texture and tone. Undercutting is used to enhance the cameo effect, along with stamping in the background.

The exterior, which is the lowest point in the carving, plays a supporting role without acting as a container for the pattern. This border is also smooth-tooled in order to contrast visually with the darker, stamped border.

Bevels are utilized along many of the edges found in the carving. These bevels are crucial if the carving is to have definition and power to it. These bevels turn an otherwise vertical edge forward, from perpendicular to the surface (90°) to between 60° and 45° to the surface.

Bevels allow the light and shadow caught by edges to be seen from the front and act as sharp lines of light and shadow around various areas in the carving. Bevels must be flat or slightly concave. Convex bevels disperse the light and the shadow, weakening their effect.

The Panel

The finished carving is about 19" in diameter, which is approximately a 250% enlargement of this pattern. Choose wood that is even-grained and consistent in color and figure. Then laminate a panel that is one inch wider and longer than the pattern to allow extra room for placing the pattern in the best spot. Remove all knots and defects from the wood before preparing it for lamination. Defects will stick out like a sore thumb in this carving.

The sapwood of each board should be placed to the front. Be sure that you laminate so the boards are oriented vertically. Your carving will look best this way. Build in some camber to help control the tendency of the panel to cup to the carved side.

I have carved this pattern as large as three feet in diameter and as small as 16" in diameter. Beyond these measurements, the design suffers. If the panel is too large, the compression of depth is too severe in 2" stock, forcing one to utilize 3" and even 4" thick wood. Too small, and the design becomes unimpressive.

You should use 2" thick stock. Besides red oak, white birch has been very successful for this carving, but any close-grained wood, especially those that are light in color, will be suitable. I have used ash, white oak, cherry, yellow birch and a number of other exotic species, too. Fine-grained woods produce a softer, gentler product, while coarse-grained woods produce bold and striking carvings.

Choose a clear, satin finish for the finished carving. Avoid staining this piece, as this will detract from the symbols.

This carving will present well in a variety of lighting conditions, but the best overall is when light crosses the panel from either side. This will cast shadow across the bevels, allowing the viewer to see the relief. The bevels do most of the work in presenting this carving to the viewer, since the toolmarking, for the most part, is quite smooth and catches little light and shadow.

Carving Hints

After the pattern is transferred to the panel using carbon paper, bandsaw the pattern to size. Then use a router to set the depths according to the pattern. Rough out the carving to the lines.

When you start modeling the figures, pay attention to the sloped areas on the hands and arms. These slopes must be carved by hand, as routers are particularly useless when it comes to doing slopes. The depths indicated for any particular area represent the highest point in that area. The figure is always modeled down to a deeper level and over the edge from that depth.

All the figures contain slopes that have to be carefully and methodically rendered. This takes time, and even a slight change in slope will affect the appearance of the finished product.

The figures are all toolmarked as smooth as possible with #2 tools and, where appropriate, skew chisels. No sanding should be done at all, just as a matter of principle. Sharp tools make sanding unnecessary and undesirable.

There is a large bevel on the edge of the stamped area that needs to be carefully and accu-rately carved. It will help separate the stamped area from the smooth-tooled border, but if it is carved out of round, it will also be a glaring reminder of careless carving.

Undercutting helps to enhance the round-ness of the figures and add visual depth to the carving. Undercut all the figures carefully and in a tidy fashion.

With the panel in an end vise, use a #2-20mm gouge to toolmark the outside edge of the carving, removing all evidence of the bandsaw. Then apply a light bevel to the corner of the outside edge.

Finish the carving, add hangers to the back, and hang it on the wall for all to enjoy.

Mare and Colt

Artist: Laurette Cissel
Dimensions: 15 1/2" by 17 1/2"
Wood: White Birch
Finish: Clear Sanding Sealer

54

About this Pattern

This has been one of the most popular patterns among my carving students, probably because it combines excellent design with a wonderful western theme. Laurette Cissel was the student who came up with the idea for a carving of a mare and a colt, and it is her design that is pictured in this book. We worked many hours on this design, bouncing our ideas off the other students in her class, who were more than happy to contribute their opinions and suggestions.

The idea of a horseshoe border is ingenious, because it extends the equestrian theme while providing a frame that is as interesting as the contents themselves. Such novel ideas can only come from the collective mind one finds in the lively and creative comradery of a carving class.

Laurette lives with her family on a rural acreage outside of town and is what we call a "country" person. She rides horses, loves animals and even works for a firm that sells animal feed, tack and medicine. This pattern, then, is close to her heart, and reflects her desire to portray her passion for country in a pleasing and meaningful way.

Laurette is what I call a "clean" carver. Not a fiber of wood is out of place in this carving, which is as smooth to the touch as it looks and shows well in almost every lighting situation. Her rendition of the subject is gentle and soft. The focus is on the relationship between the mare and its colt rather than on the details of anatomy and horse hardware.

The Panel

To use this design you will have to first enlarge the pattern so that it is roughly 15$1/2$" wide and 17$1/2$" tall. Use a photocopier and scale it to a 200% enlargement. Then prepare a relief panel approximately 16$1/2$" wide by 18$1/2$" tall onto which you will copy this pattern using carbon tracing paper. The panel should be a full inch wider and taller than the pattern to allow you to position the pattern properly on the panel. Build a bit of camber into the panel for stability.

Note that the depth indicated for the horseshoe frame is "top" at the upper left, and $5/8$" at the

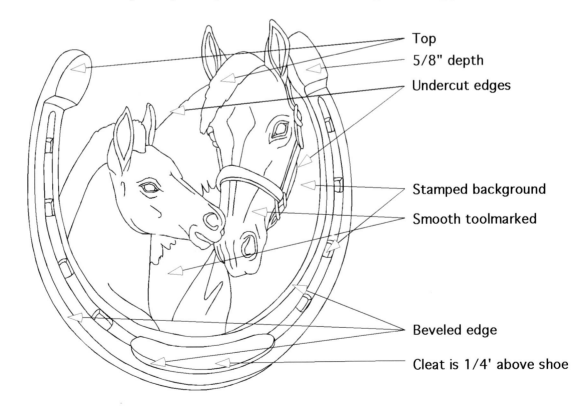

Top
5/8" depth
Undercut edges
Stamped background
Smooth toolmarked
Beveled edge
Cleat is 1/4' above shoe

upper right. This indicates that the horseshoe slopes gently downward from the upper left to the lower right, until it terminates behind the ear of the mare. A router can be used to assist in implementing these slopes by routering the depths where indicated on the pattern. However, the final slope will have to be carved by hand.

Carving Hints

Manes are carved using a #12-3mm v-tool, with a #12-6mm or #12-8mm v-tool to make the notches along the edges of the manes. Be sure to model the mane somewhat, using a #9-7mm gouge and a #9-5mm gouge so that it does not look flat and lifeless when the hair texture is applied.

Undercutting should be applied around each of the horses, even along the top edge of the carving where the boundary of the animals form the perimeter of the carving. However, the horseshoe should not be undercut.

The horseshoe is carved so that it appears to be viewed from the left side. This means you will have to slope the outside edge of the horseshoe carefully in order to reinforce the illusion of perspective. The width of the sloped area and the angle of the slope vary as you move from one end of the shoe to another. Likewise, the cleat has a variable bevel along its lower edge.

The groove in the horseshoe contains eight holes where the shoe nails would be inserted. The bottom of the nail holes are stamped the same as the background behind the horses. The sides of the grooves are beveled more on one side than the other to assist in the rendering of perspective.

Stamping should be applied to the background behind the mare. Be sure to stamp the undercut area and to keep your stamping consistent and as close to saturation as possible without pulverizing the wood.

Use a #9-10mm gouge to shape the musculature of the animals on the neck and a #7-10mm gouge for the face. These grooves will be softened and blended by the tools you use for final tool-marking.

Use a #3-5mm gouge to apply the final toolmarking to the body of both the mare and the colt. Overlap each cut so the surface is consistent and smooth. You can orient your toolmarks so they accentuate the shape of the horses, and help define the musculature.

Old Crusty

Artist: Kevin Dewhirst
Dimensions: 13" by 18"
Wood: Black Cherry
Finish: Clear Sanding Sealer

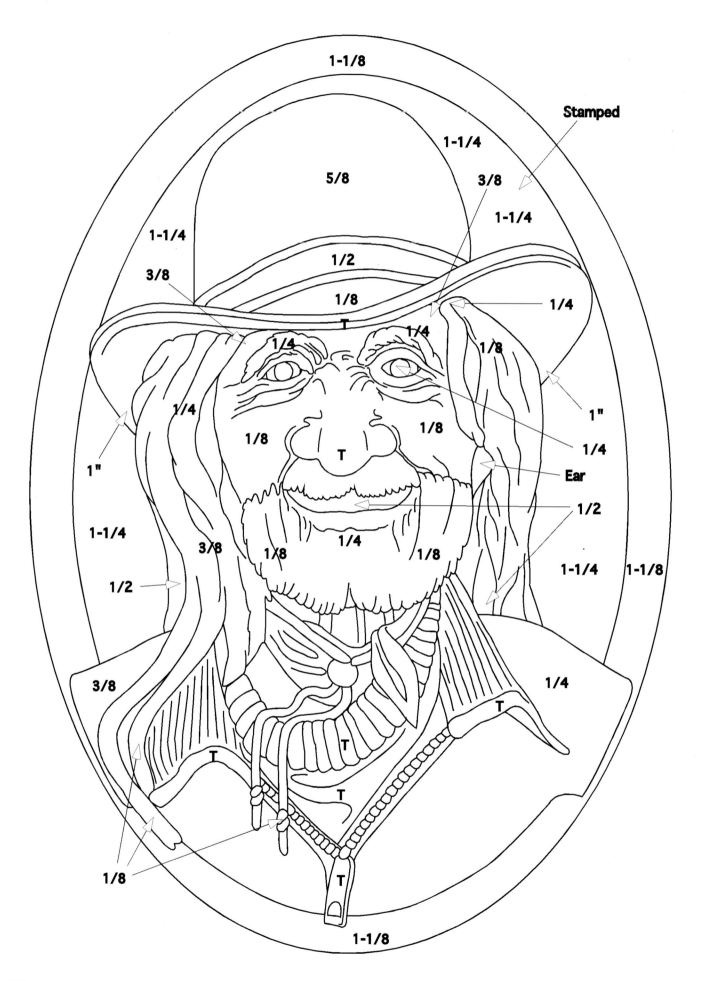

58

About this Pattern

This delightful carving by one of my students, Kevin Dewhirst, was completed some years ago in carving class. It depicts an old man, somewhat worse for wear, but evidently content with his meager lot in life. His long hair, toothless grin and well-worn clothes speak to his lack of concern about personal hygiene. His leather hat is probably his most prized possession. But his smile is endearing and his eyes twinkle with mischief, making him a most lovable character.

I think I have met a few "Old Crustys" in my day. They tend to be what the community categorizes as "colorful characters," on the margins of society, but neither accepted or scorned, and certainly harmless.

Kevin chose to do this piece in 2" black cherry. He made a good choice, as this wood holds excellent detail, and its color suits the subject very well. Kevin insists that this is not a self portrait. <grin>

Once again, the cameo format used in this carving has produced a striking portrait, with open borders that support, rather than contain the pattern. To have a high-sided frame on this picture would be less than desirable.

Besides the "Wolf Portrait," this pattern is probably the most difficult in this book, mainly because of the level of detail, but also due to the fact that this is a frontal human portrait. Portraits are much easier when done in profile. Frontal portraits demand a high degree of control over the dimension of depth, which must be carefully compressed so as to render the figure realistically. And since we all know what a human face should look like, it is hard to get away with mistakes in perspective and detail.

Most of the facial features move between the depths indicated as high points for a particular area in the pattern. You will have to study the photo to understand how surfaces slope and curve into one another.

There is a wonderful variety of texture throughout this relief, from the zipper to the top of the leather hat. The inside of the jacket collar is corduroy, while the turtleneck sweater is ribbed. Note also how the inside of the mouth is stamped, to darken it and separate it visually from the rest of the face.

It should be relatively easy for you to duplicate the hair, as the photo clearly shows the high points and low points, and the direction of the tooling.

The toughest areas of the carving to do well are the eyes and nose. Get these right and your carving will succeed. Get them wrong, and whatever else you have done right will count for nothing. The pupils here have been rendered with v-grooves rather than with the classic method of carving the pupils hollow. You may choose whichever method you prefer, but I recommend the pupils be hollowed. This is the only variation from the pattern that will definitely improve your carving. But please practice an eye on a scrap of wood before making the permanent cuts in this carving.

You should approach this carving with patience and perseverance, knowing that it was carved by a regular person like yourself. Careful observation and a methodical approach to rendering will result in a beautiful finished carving.

The Panel

The finished carving is about 13" by 18", which is approximately a 190% enlargement of this pattern. If you prefer a slightly larger panel, a 200% enlargement of the pattern will do nicely. Choose wood that is even grained and consistent in color and figure.

Place the sapwood to the front, and laminate so the boards are oriented vertically. Try to build some camber into the panel to help control the tendency of the panel to cup to the carved side. Use 2" thick stock. Choose a clear, satin finish for the completed carving.

This carving would also look very fine in

maple, yellow birch, alder and mahogany, all of which are fine-grained and a little darker in color than white birch, which I use for most of my carvings. Still, cherry is simply beautiful, don't you think?

The best overall place to hang this carving is where light crosses it from either side. This will cast shadow across the various textures, most of which are primarily vertical, allowing the viewer to see the relief clearly. There are not many bevels in this carving, seeing that most of the edges are rounded over.

Carving Hints

After the pattern is transferred to the panel using carbon paper, bandsaw the panel to size. Use a router to set the depths according to the pattern, but only in the area of the top of the hat, the two shoulders, the chest area and the background. Avoid using the router in the face areas, as these are best left to handwork with sharp tools. When the waste wood around the figure is removed, you can rough out the figure to the lines.

When you start modeling the figure, pay attention to the sloped areas on the face, hair and garments. These slopes vary constantly, requiring you to refer to the photo continuously. The pattern indicates, with arrows pointing to specific points on the carving, the depths for those areas. Adjoining areas slope downward to meet these depths.

Do not attempt to texture the hair or the collars of the jacket and the sweater until they are shaped properly. This would be like placing the cart before the horse.

The hair is tooled with a #12-3mm v-tool, and notched along the edges to make it look lifelike. The face is smoothly tooled with a #3-8mm gouge before the creases are applied with a 90° v-tool or a #12-3mm veiner.

Toolmark the hat under the brim and above the head band with a #7-10mm gouge, attempting to keep your cuts short and consistent.

Undercut the figure carefully and in a tidy fashion. Some of the edges within the figure are also undercut, for example, the beard and the edge of the coat collar.

The inside and outside edge of the smooth-tooled border have bevels applied to them, to help separate them from the stamped texture of the background.

With the panel secured in an end vise, use a #2-20mm gouge to toolmark the outside edge of the carving, removing all evidence of the bandsaw. Then apply a light bevel to the corner of the outside edge.

Finish the carving with a clear sealer according to the SSW method.

Scroll

Artist: W.F. (Bill) Judt
Dimensions: 18½" by 24"
Wood: White Birch
Finish: Clear Sanding Sealer

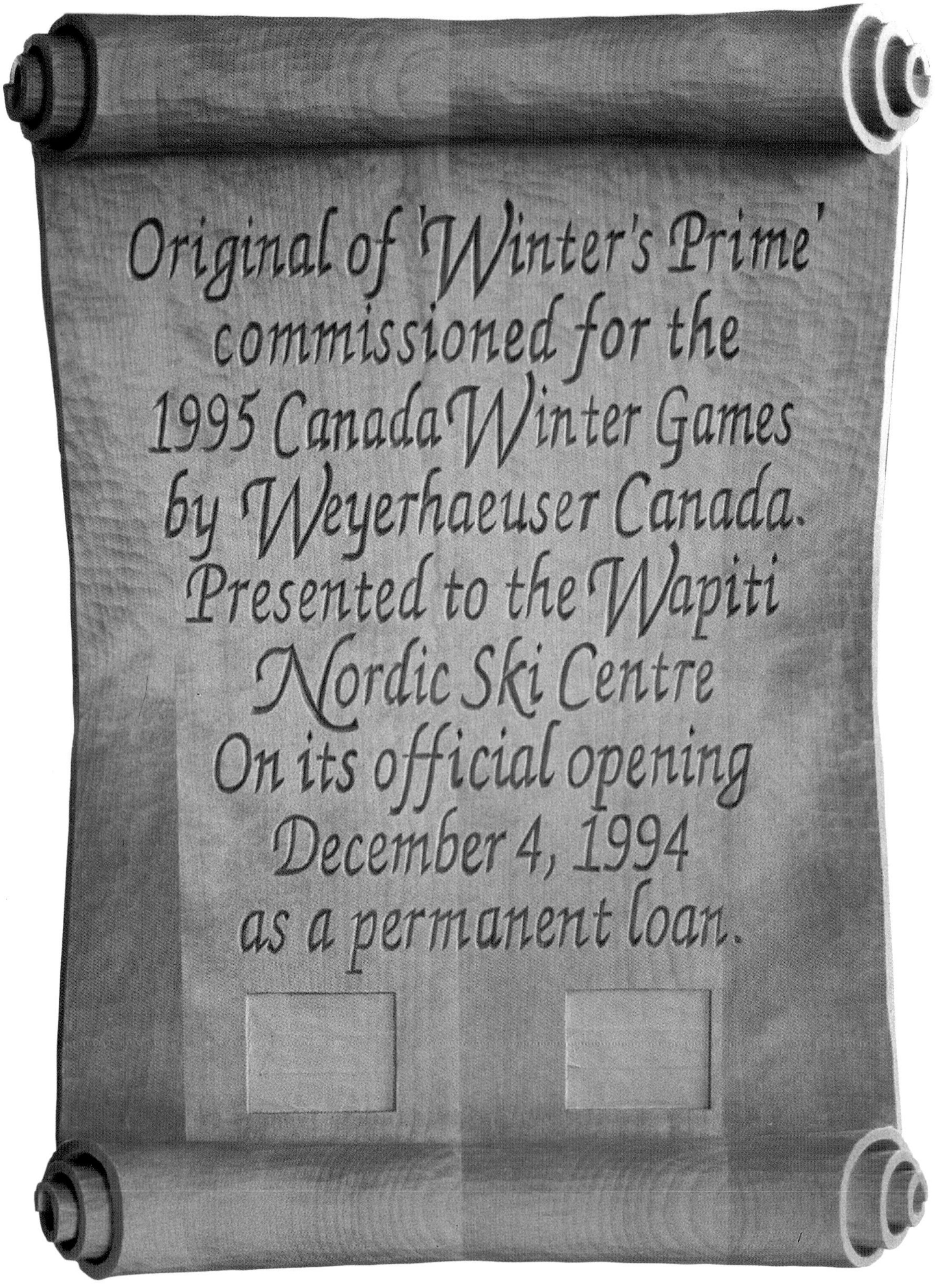

Original of 'Winter's Prime'
commissioned for the
1995 Canada Winter Games
by Weyerhaeuser Canada.
Presented to the Wapiti
Nordic Ski Centre
On its official opening
December 4, 1994
as a permanent loan.

Top 1/8 Top

7/8 7/8

7/8 7/8

ABCDEFG
HIJKLMNO
PQRSTUV
WXYZ

1"

abcdefg
hijklmno
pqrstuv
wxyz

7/8 7/8

Top 1/8 Top

62

About this Pattern

This pattern is one of my own. A while back, I was approached by the Canada Winter Games committee to carve a scroll which would hang beside a large oil painting purchased for the Wapiti Nordic Ski Centre, a modern cross-country skiing facility just outside of Grande Prairie, Alberta. The purpose of this scroll is purely functional. It is not meant to be a piece of art. However, it certainly was meant to look attractive as it made its proclamation.

I think this is a very useful pattern for those who wish to make a statement or carve their favorite poem or passage of sacred scripture. It can be used for dedications, proclamations, memorials and the like.

Notice that there are two brass plates under the text. These were for official Winter Games and Sponsor logos. Part of the function of this scroll was to point to the painting, and the other function was to recognize the sponsors of the painting.

I chose a classical decorative rendition of a scroll for this carving. Normally one would not expect a scroll to roll up the way this one does, with the ends of both sides visible from the front. One would expect only one side to be visible at a time. I carved the scroll this way because it is has a more balanced appearance than a more realistically carved scroll and looks far more attractive.

You will also notice that the color photo contains different text than the pattern, and less detail as well. It seemed silly to include in the pattern the words of dedication you see in the photo and more reasonable and useful to include an alphabet in a calligraphic font for your convenience, should you wish to use this pattern. This font carves well, especially when it is incised and adds to the decorative appearance of the scroll.

The photo does not contain any cracks along its edges like you see in the pattern. These cracks were an afterthought and will serve to make the scroll look older and more distinguished.

Note the consistent use of bevels along all the outside edges of the scroll. These bevels not only strengthen the edges so they are not easily damaged, but they also help define the carving by catching light and shadow. Without these bevels, the scroll looks weak and unimportant.

The scroll detail (top, side and end views) will help you understand how to carve the curls in this scroll. The side view shows that the scroll's depth is somewhat compressed. The end view shows that the curls slope inward and that undercutting is used to hide the unused thickness of the panel.

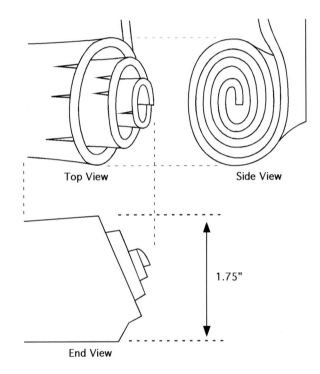

Top View · Side View · End View · 1.75"

The top view gives you an idea of how the curl should appear to the viewer's eye. It is a complex shape that can baffle you for a while, like it did me. But it is also a logical shape, based on a spiral, as the side view illustrates. You must approach the carving of these curls logically and systematically. All views show that the curl has a continuous bevel, undercut to accentuate the thinness of the scroll. The little cracks are added as a final detail after the curls and scroll have received their final toolmarking.

The Panel

The finished carving can be whatever size you wish. The one I carved was about 18½" by 24" which is approximately a 240% enlargement of this pattern. Laminate a panel that is one inch wider and longer than the pattern to allow extra room for placing the pattern in the best spot. Be sure that you laminate so the boards are oriented vertically, as this makes for the most attractive finished product.

You should use 2" thick stock, unless the scroll you intend to carve is very close to the actual size of the pattern in this book. In that case, 1½" thick stock is adequate. I used white birch for this carving, but any close-grained wood, especially those lighter in color, will be suitable. Avoid coarse grained woods like oak and ash, or dark woods like black walnut. The former is too coarse, and the grain will compete with the relief for visibility. The latter is too dark and will not show properly under most normal lighting conditions.

Choose a clear, satin finish for the completed carving. I use a sanding sealer basecoat and a topcoat of paste wax, according to the SSW method. But a quality oil finish, spray lacquer or varnish would work well too. They are just more difficult to apply and control than the SSW method.

Carving Hints

After the pattern is transferred to the panel, use a bandsaw to remove the wood along the perimeter. Then use a router (a plunge router is the best here) to set the depths between the top and bottom curls, where the text will ultimately be placed. The router should be set to ⁷⁄₈" only, as the interior of the scroll slopes gradually downward another ⅛" from the sides to the center. This slope needs to be carved by hand and smoothed before carbon paper can be used to trace the text onto the wood.

After the inside of the scroll has been shaped and smoothed, you are ready to carve the end-curls. These are tricky little things to carve. Keep in mind that you must first set each layer of the curl to its own specific depth. The curls are separated from each other by about ⅛", and the thickness of each scroll as it curls around is about ⅛". These add up to about ¼" depth for each layer of the curl.

When carving the curls, be sure to observe their emerging shape from the top, the sides and the ends in order to ensure that none of these views is distorted.

The undercutting of the scroll curls is very important for achieving a realistic appearance. The top view shows how the undercutting works.

The curls get toolmarked horizontally (left to right) with even, shallow gouges, using, perhaps a #5-5mm gouge. The same applies to the outside body of the curls. This toolmarking is coarser than the shallow, flat toolmarking applied to the body of the text area with a #2-20mm gouge.

The bevels on the edge of each curl are at about a 60° angle, sloping downward more than sideways. These bevels must be cleanly carved and flat-surfaced or slightly concave rather than convex. This is so that the edges of the bevels are sharp in order to reflect clean, sharp light and shadow.

The body of the scroll must also be undercut, though near the end of the carving process rather than earlier. If you undercut too early, it will be difficult to hold the panel with bench-dogs, the sloping sides working against the clamping action.

Finally, I attached a stand to the back of my scroll with screws, which allowed the scroll to stand on a flat surface on its own. The stand can be removed if and when the scroll needs to be mounted on the wall. You might want to do the same.

The most difficult part of this carving is the curls, but the most risky part of this carving is the lettering, especially if you have lots of it. Incised lettering allows for no errors. Make a mistake with the text and be prepared to cut out the offending strip of wood and laminate a new piece in its place. So, be careful. Practice first on some scrap wood and eliminate all distractions when you carve. Prayer helps too. <grin>

Wolf Portrait

Artist: W.F. (Bill) Judt
Dimensions: 18" by 21"
Wood: White Birch
Finish: Clear Sanding Sealer

3/8

3/8

3/4

1-1/4

1-1/4

1-1/4

1-1/4

1-1/4

3/8

3/8

3/8

3/8

3/8

3/8

3/8

3/8

3/8

3/8

3/8

3/8

3/8

3/8

3/8

3/4

3/4

3/4

3/4

3/4

3/4

3/4

1/4

1/4

1/4

1/4

1/8

1/8

1/8

1/8

1/2

5/8

5/8

5/8

5/8

5/8

T

T

T

T

T

Concave

Concave

About this Pattern

This wolf is sizing you up. His penetrating eyes are calculating the risk and estimating the benefit of standing his ground, maybe even advancing toward you. His ears are perked forward, listening for audible clues that tell of danger or weakness. Behind, the spruce boughs surround him like the forest that is his home, framing his thickly furred body. If you move to the side, his eyes follow. He stands motionless, solid, confident, mysterious.

One of the most potent symbols of the wilderness and of cunning and stealth, the wolf has long been a favorite subject for artists. With this portrait you will be able to capture that symbol in wood and at the same time gain valuable clues as to how to create patterns for yourself of other wild creatures.

There is more depth crammed into this carving than any other in this book. If you were to put a ruler across the top of the face, you would be surprised to see how shallow the depths are from the tip of the nose to the tips of the ears.

Most of the face is carved in less than $1/8"$ depth. Some of the modeling is as shallow as $1/16"$. It is very important , therefore, to accentuate what little actual relief exists with directional toolmarking, in order to lead the eye of the viewer to assume shape and form. As with the Dall's Sheep, most of the facial features move between the depths indicated on the pattern. You will have to study the photo to understand how surfaces slope and curve into one another. Routering should not take place within the boundaries of the wolf's body, since these areas must be hand modeled to their depths.

It should be relatively easy for you to duplicate the fur, as the photo clearly shows the high points and low points and the direction of the tooling. Remember that there are very few straight lines in the fur, if any. Most lines are some variation of the classic S-curve. The S-curve allows you to move from one area over a slope into the adjoining area easily. The S-curve also allows you to disguise a flat area so it appears either rippled with muscle or covered with thick fur.

The layers of fur must be carved so they remain distinct from each other. This is done by roughing the edges of each fur area using a v-tool and a judicious bit of undercutting.

One of the nice features of this carving is the hollow pupils which appear to follow you as you move sideways in front of the carving. Another is the concave stamped background, which provides a neutral texture and color behind the wolf so as not to distract from the animal's contours.

I chose a repeating pattern of spruce boughs to ornament the carving. These are relatively straight forward to carve. Of course, the spruce boughs echo the texture of the wolf, suggesting that in nature the animal blends into its surroundings like a ghost in fog.

The background behind the spruce boughs is deliberately plain so that the boughs stand out clearly. It is toolmarked smooth because another area of stamping would have been redundant.

All in all, this is a powerful carving, and one that will surely be a challenge to carve and a delight to display in your home.

The Panel

The finished carving is about 18" by 21", which is approximately a 225% enlargement of this pattern. Choose wood that is even-grained and consistent in color and figure, placing the sapwood to the front, and laminating so the boards are oriented vertically. Building some camber into the panel will help control the tendency of the panel to cup to the carved side. Use stock that is a full 2" thick.

This carving is done in yellow birch and has been finished with a clear coat of sanding sealer using the SSW method.

The best overall place to hang this carving is where light crosses it from either side.

Carving Hints

When you start modeling the figures, pay attention to the sloped areas on the face, forehead, eye brows and neck. These slopes vary constantly, requiring you to refer to the photo continuously. Some of the fur areas are separated by stop cuts, even some slight undercutting. Most other areas blend smoothly into adjoining areas that are similarly toolmarked. Do not attempt to texture the fur on the wolf until the underlying body is shaped properly.

Undercutting is essential to the appearance of the wolf, although it is a relatively straight-forward procedure. Concave undercuts are more convincing and are accomplished by raising the handle of the tool as the cutting edge moves toward the background. Convex undercuts happen when the handle is lowered while undercutting takes place. Bevels in this carving are used along the edges of the outside border and along the eyelids. The rest of the edges are rounded over, with the toolmarking following over the edges.

The fur areas are initially modeled with gouges until their shape approximates the photo. Then you are ready to use a medium #12-8mm v-tool to carve the deepest grooves and a #12-3mm v-tool to add the finer fur textures. As a finishing touch, vertical notches along the edges of the ears and the fur layers of the neck make the wolf look more lifelike. The last thing you want to do with the perimeter of the wolf's body is to end up with a smooth edge. The edge must be notched to indicate the fur moving from the front, to the side and, finally, around the edge of the animal.

The spruce boughs should be modeled cleanly before attempting to apply texture with a #12-6mm or #12-8mm v-tool. There is a center line that meanders around the boughs from which all the v-tooling moves to either the inside or the outside of the boughs. Once a pleasing pattern of v-grooves has been applied to their surface, the boughs need to be notched along their edges in the same manner as the fur on the wolf.

The hollow edge of the stamped area should be a true radius, that is, based on the arc of a circle. The stamping moves from the flat background up the sides of this concave edge, up to the bevel separating the flat border and the stamped background. Be sure to stamp under the undercut edges of the wolf as well.

With the panel in an end vise, use a #2-20mm gouge to toolmark the outside edge of the carving, removing all evidence of the bandsaw. Then apply a light bevel to the corner of the outside edge.

Finish the carving with a clear sealer according to the SSW method. Enjoy!

Elephant

Artist: Louw Smit
Dimensions: 15½" by 17"
Wood: White Birch
Finish: Clear Sanding Sealer

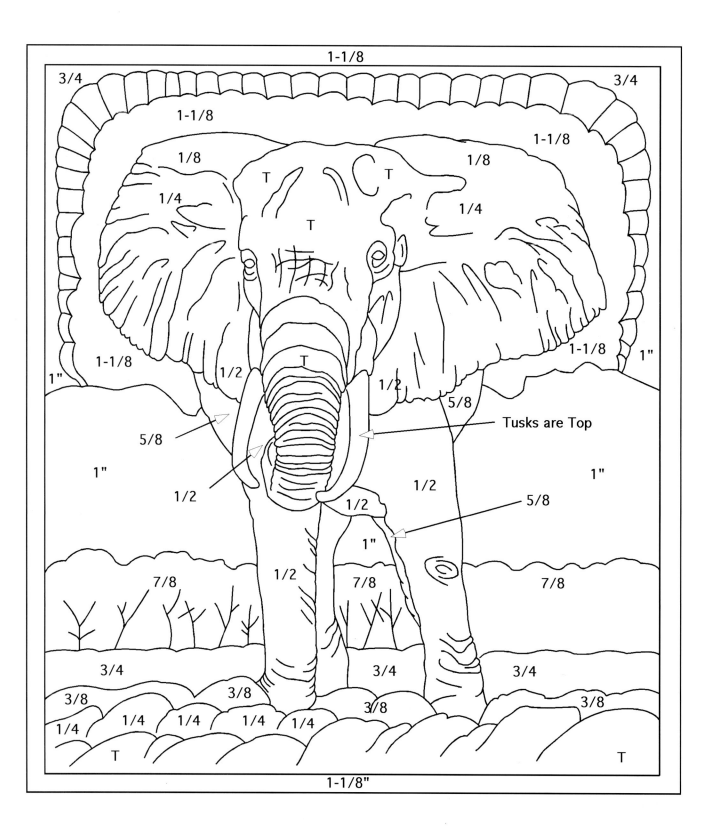

Tusks are Top

About this Pattern

This pattern was developed in my studio for one of my carving students. The student's name is Louw Smit, and he works as a psychiatrist at the local hospital. Formerly a resident of South Africa, Louw (pronounced "low" as in "hello") intends to carve a series of same-size reliefs on African animals for his home, this elephant carving being the first.

His carving features a high degree of compression in the depth dimension, up to 20:1. The entire depth of the elephant is rendered in only 1" of relief, making it necessary to properly layer the figure so that perspective can be achieved. The horizon of the carving is deliberately low so that the elephant appears huge and dominating. The border is recessed to allow the carving to be fit into a frame at a later date.

Note how the elephant is the most detailed element of the carving. In contrast, the foreground grass, the middle-ground shrubs and background landscape are stylized and reduced in detail to give the elephant the primary focus in the carving. Even the sky and clouds are means by which to enhance the elephant's prominence in the pattern.

The Panel

The finished carving is about $15\frac{1}{2}$" by 17", which is approximately a 220% enlargement of this pattern. Laminate a panel that is one inch wider and longer than the pattern to allow extra room for placing the pattern in the best spot. Be sure that you laminate so the boards are oriented vertically.

You should use 2" thick stock. White birch was used for this carving, but any close-grained wood, especially those lighter in color, will be suitable.

Choose a clear, satin finish for the completed carving. Louw used a clear sanding sealer basecoat with a topcoat of paste wax, according to the SSW method. A cream-wax stain (shoe cream) will also work very well with this carving and allow you to choose a color to match the decor of the room in which it will hang.

Carving Hints

After the pattern is transferred to the panel using carbon paper, bandsaw the pattern to size. Then use a router to set the depths according to the pattern.

Most of the elephant's face, trunk and legs are essentially flat, having been rounded slightly only near the edges. The appearance of roundness and shape are made possible in part by effective tool-marking in these areas. Use directional toolmarking, that is, orient your toolmarks on the face, trunk and legs so that they follow the shape and contours of these areas.

The legs are toolmarked with a #5-5mm gouge, the face and trunk with a #2-8mm gouge. The grooves on the trunk are carved with a #12-3mm v-tool, and the edges of the v-grooves are softened slightly with a small, shallow gouge.

A variety of #5, #7 and #9 gouges will be needed to shape the inside of the ears, which are covered with overlapping hills and valleys. Be sure to carve vertical grooves along the edge of the ears to add variety to their appearance. Smooth-edged ears would look rather artificial.

The top layers of grass are textured with a #11-3mm veiner, while the vertical layer of grass directly behind them is carved with a small v-tool. Note how this layer is notched on the top edge with v-cuts. This adds realism to the grass.

Horizontal toolmarks are applied to the last two layers of background behind the elephant. Once this texturing is complete, the tree branches can be cut in with a small v-tool.

The cloud effect around the inside of the cloud layer is done in two stages. The first stage is to rough out the shapes, and the second is to apply smooth toolmarks to the hollows, leaving the edges between hollows sharp and even.

Stamping is applied to the deepest background behind the elephant to finish off the texturing process. Bevels can be applied to all border areas. You are then ready to finish the carving with your choice of the SSW method or a cream-wax stain.

Mary

Artist: W.F. (Bill) Judt
Dimensions: 16½" by 23
Wood: Eastern (Yellow) Birch
Finish: Clear Sanding Sealer

Relief Carving

The Ascending Lord

Slope the sides of the letters so they appear extruded from the background

Top

Border to be stamped

1"

1/8

1/4

7/8

7/8

Letters at 3/4" depth, or 1/4" above border

1/4

7/8

7/8

Behold I am the Handmaid of the Lord

1"

1"

1"

1"

1"

1"

T

T

T

T

T

T

This surface curves from the 1/2" level down to the 7/8" level

Interior border at 1/2"

Treasury of Patterns

About this Pattern

In Christian circles, this image of Mary strikes a responsive chord, primarily because Mary is a strong symbol of womanhood, motherhood and obedient service to her Lord. I developed this design in response to a commission from a local Catholic priest who wanted the carving as a gift for his elderly mother. It was his way of showing his respect, love and gratitude for her devotion to him over the years.

The idea here was to render Mary as a young woman on the threshold of the challenges of motherhood, yet to render her also as strong, pure of heart and decidedly committed to her calling. Some images of Mary suggest weakness, uncertainty or fragility. Or they might suggest that Mary was something other than an ordinary woman blessed with an extraordinary calling. This pattern clearly portrays her as typical of what womanhood is about.

The surrounding text declares her promise to accept the path chosen for her life without reservation. Text adds a dimension to the carving that extends and enhances the impact of the image. Without the words, the carving falls flat.

The Panel

To use this design, enlarge the pattern on the previous page so that it is roughly 16½" wide and 23" tall. Use a photocopier and scale it to 275%. Then prepare a relief panel approximately 17½" wide and 24" tall onto which you will copy this pattern using carbon tracing paper. The panel should be a full inch wider in width and height to allow you room to place the pattern properly onto the panel.

Note that the background behind Mary curves gently down from the interior border, the toolmarks oriented to the center of the figure. The interior border is ½" below the figure, but ¼" above the stamped text border. It is toolmarked smooth, with light bevels on both edges to soften and tidy it up.

Carving Hints

The surfaces of the figure are carved using a #3-5mm or #3-8mm gouge, leaving toolmarks that overlap so as to leave no remnants of the un-tooled surfaces. The idea is to give the figure a clean, consistent texture that will unify the design and allow for a consistent reflective value over the entire figure. Be sure to orient the toolmarks so they accentuate the shape and flow of the figure. You can see how this is done in the photo.

The surfaces of the text are also carved cleanly, but with a #2-8mm or #2-12mm gouge. After they are tooled, slight bevels are applied to the edges of each letter, to soften their appearance and tidy them up.

The letters are meant to look like they extrude from the background. To do this, you must carve the letters so their sides are sloped outward from the top to the bottom at an angle between 10% and 15%. Besides making the letters look bolder, this technique greatly strengthens the letters, allowing the delicate serifs to be carved confidently.

The face, feet, and hands of the figure should be a little smoother than the garment so that they can be distinguished more easily. If you wish to use a very small scraper to smooth these areas after you have toolmarked them, that is perfectly acceptable.

The outside perimeter of the carving needs to be tooled with a #2-16mm or #3-20mm gouge. Bevels need to be applied to the top and bottom edges of the perimeter to clean then up.

Mary's hair needs a small veiner, say a #11-3mm gouge, to give the correct effect. A #8-4mm and a #8-10mm gouge are used to model (shape) the garment prior to final toolmarking. The hands, feet and garment are detailed with a #12-3mm v-tool.

Most of the edges found on the garment have some form of bevel applied. Bevels, more than any other final detail, clarify the image, allowing sharp vertical edges to soften, turning them forward so they are visible to the viewer. Start with thin bevels, and widen them as required. Use a #1-12mm skew to apply the bevels, and make sure they are never flatter than 45 degrees. Generally, bevels need to be applied at angles between 45° and 60°.

Apply sanding sealer and wax, as per the SSW method.

NEW WOODWORKING TITLES

Available at your favorite book supplier!

**MAKING TOYS:
HEIRLOOM CARS AND
TRUCKS TO BUILD**
*by Sam Martin
and Roger Schroeder*
1-56523-079-5
$14.95

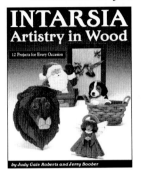

**INTARSIA:
ARTISTRY IN WOOD**
by Judy Gale Roberts

1-56523-096-5
$14.95

**CHRISTMAS SCROLL SAW
PATTERNS AND DESIGNS**
by Tom Zieg

1-56523-093-0
$12.95

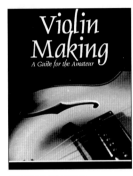

**VIOLIN MAKING
FOR THE AMATEUR**
by Bruce Ossman

1-56523-091-4
$14.95

**CARVING SIGNS:
THE WOODWORKERS
GUIDE TO LETTERING,
CARVING AND GILDING**
*by Greg Krochta
and Roger Schroeder*
1-56523-078-7
$24.95 (August)

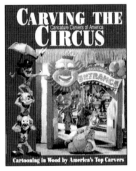

**CARVING THE CCA
CIRCUS - CARTOONING
IN WOOD**
by America's Top Carvers

1-56523-094-9
$19.95

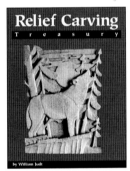

**RELIEF CARVING
TREASURY**
by Bill Judt

1-56523-097-3
$14.95

**CARVING TROPHY
DEER AND ELK**
by Todd Swaim

1-56523-089-2
$19.95

CARVING SPOONS
by Shirley Adler

1-56523-092-2
$14.95

**REALISTIC DUCK CARVING-
A STEP-BY-STEP
ILLUSTRATED MANUAL**
by Alfred Ponte

1-56523-086-8
$9.95

**COLLAPSIBLE BASKET
PATTERNS - OVER 100
DESIGNS FOR SCROLL
SAW/BANDSAW**
by Rick Longabaugh
1-56523-087-6
$12.95

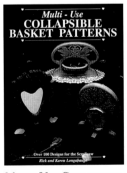

**MULTI-USE COLLAPSIBLE
BASKET PATTERNS -
OVER 100 DESIGNS/
SCROLL SAW**
by Rick Longabaugh
1-56523-088-4
$12.95

 **Fox Chapel Publishing Co., Inc. • 1970 Broad Street • East Petersburg, PA 17520**
1-800-457-9112 • 717-560-4702 Fax

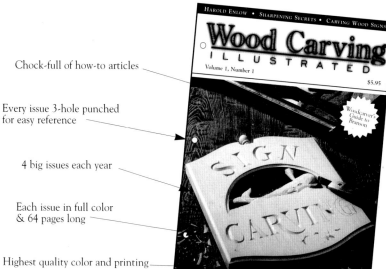